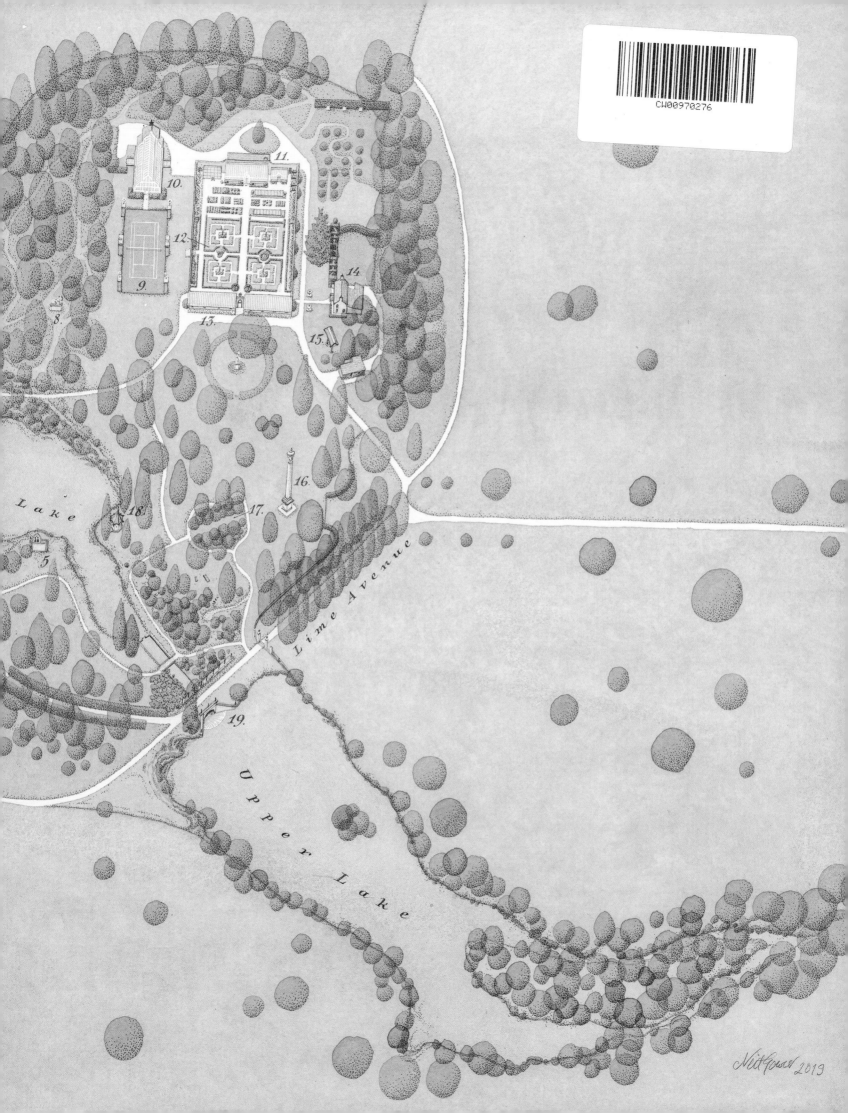

Lake

Lime Avenue

Upper Lake

5

8.

9.

10.

11.

12.

13.

14.

15.

16.

17.

18.

19.

Neil Gower 2013

FOR

SEBASTIAN

JEREMY MUSSON

HENBURY

AN EXTRAORDINARY HOUSE

FOREWORD BY
HRH THE PRINCE OF WALES

PIMPERNEL PRESS
MMXIX

PIMPERNEL PRESS LTD

www.pimpernelpress.com

A catalogue record for this book
is available from the British Library.

ISBN 978-1-910258-11-8

Designed by Dalrymple
Typeset in ATF Garamond and MVB Solitaire
Printed and bound in China by
C&C Offset Printing Company Limited

A NOTE ON NAMES

The creator of Henbury Hall shares his name with his
grandfather, the inventor Sebastian Ziani de Ferranti. In these pages,
in order to distinguish between the two, I have called the inventor
Sebastian Ziani de Ferranti, or Ziani de Ferranti, and his grandson,
builder of Henbury, Sebastian de Ferranti, or Sebastian.

Jeremy Musson

ENDPAPERS Neil Gower's plan of the Hall,
gardens and grounds at Henbury, drawn in 2019.

PAGE ONE Sebastian de Ferranti's personal bookplate,
drawn by Graham Rust, incorporating an Arcadian landscape, his helicopter,
and (bottom right) the plumed helmet from his period
as a cavalry officer.

FRONTISPIECE Henbury Hall from the west: a classical building
in a classical landscape.

CONTENTS

It gives me great pleasure to introduce this splendid volume, celebrating Sebastian de Ferranti's legacy at Henbury Hall. Henbury Hall represents Sebastian's single-minded dedication to what he believed in – that a house should be an expression of the best design, craftsmanship, decoration and comfort.

Of course, the design of Henbury was inspired by the great master Palladio and by the English 18th Century country house tradition and the work of Sir John Vanbrugh. It was also inspired by the landscape in which it sits – that very traditional, open parkland which Sebastian loved so much.

I can recall with great fondness my visits to Henbury – not least my first. On an extremely chilly day in February I was invited to lay the foundation stone from which, as I tapped it with a large wooden gavel, a small piece of stone broke off the corner. Harry Jocelyn, long-serving Professor of Classics at the University of Manchester, composed a suitable Latin motto to commemorate the event: "lapidem primum henburii carolus princeps walliae 1985 posuit ac fregit", which in modern English is "This first stone of Henbury was laid by Charles, Prince of Wales, 1985 – and broken."

The glory of Henbury is how cleverly Julian Bicknell, and all those involved, made the house the best it could be; and how the house manages to be both a glorious expression of the Palladian tradition and a comfortable country house. Julian was very much involved in my Institute of Architecture, as it was known in those days, and I was delighted to witness at first hand the extraordinary contribution that he made to this wonderful project.

Sebastian was a 20th Century English gentleman, proud of his own Italian descent and of his career in British industry. He loved the countryside and country sports, was a dedicated equestrian and a philanthropist, all of which he carried with a light touch. He also had a remarkable eye for detail, so Henbury Hall expressed his love of fine things and the pleasures of the English country house tradition.

I am delighted that this book provides an insight into Sebastian's vision and legacy, celebrating his life and passions.

AS A GARDENER, I AM CONSTANTLY AWARE OF HOW THE TINIEST seed grows into the most beautiful flower, every part perfectly created. This analogy can perhaps be fittingly applied to this book.

I can vividly recall the day several years ago when I came in from the garden at Henbury and said to Sebastian in the most casual way, almost thinking out loud, that I thought I would write a journal of the garden and all the considerable changes we were making in it at that time.

My intention was that the journal should be purely for our own interest and be useful as a record both for ourselves and for any who gardened here after us. The idea was greeted by my husband with great enthusiasm, with him adding that, while I was doing that, I could also write about the house! My reply was that he should do the part on the house himself, as it was, after all, he who had built it. It was a light-hearted conversation at the time, almost a joke between us, but the idea – the seed – had been planted and it had taken root.

In truth, we both loved the idea and referred often to 'our book', which became a mythical entity shimmering somewhere in the future. Often a conversation would end with 'and we must remember to put that in the book', and, when we remembered, brief notes about different aspects of house or garden were scribbled down and popped in a folder ready for the day we got down to actually writing the book.

Sadly, thinking and talking was as far as we got. To my sorrow, Sebastian died and that appeared to be the end of that. But somehow that little seed was still there and germinating. The more I thought about it, the more I thought what an extraordinary thing Sebastian had done in building Henbury Hall – extraordinary and remarkable and brave – and how it would honour his memory to record it well for future generations to read about.

Just as this book was born from a thought, so Henbury Hall was born from Sebastian's dream. From the very beginning the idea was his. He pursued his dream with courage and unstinting attention to every detail and brought everyone along with him, creating what Jeremy refers to in the book as his 'ministry of all the talents'.

The result is an extraordinary and beautiful house, built against all the odds in our present utilitarian age, providing a beacon of beauty, a dream perfectly manifested, and a powerful response to the unnecessary ugliness of much modern architecture.

The little seed to write the book persisted, but now the reasons for doing so were different. This would sadly no longer be a book Sebastian and I wrote together, but one I resolved to write for him, to applaud his great achievement (which I jokingly used to tell him was his ticket for heaven).

In comparison to the great country houses of England, Henbury is very small fry indeed, but what it stands for is, I believe, great in its own way. It is, of course, an example of perfect skill from architect to upholsterer, but more than that, it stands for one man's courage and determination to live the way he wanted to, and in doing so to shine a light of beauty in a world that is often dark.

And so the tiny seed planted all those years ago has finally come to flower. This would never have happened without Jeremy Musson, who thankfully, when I asked him, agreed to write the book. He has been a tower of strength, pulling together all the strands to make a cohesive story and achieving a brilliant result and one which I know Sebastian would have been delighted with. My grateful thanks go to him, without whom it would all still be just a thought.

I hope people will enjoy the book, the wonderful pictures and the elegant design, which create in effect a biography of this beautifully crafted house in both text and image, and enjoy the tour through its history, its architectural form, its interiors and also in its gardens – which have been my personal joy, and in which Sebastian and I spent so many happy hours.

Gilly Liani de Ferranti

HENBURY · APRIL 2019

CHAPTER I

HENBURY: A HOUSE IN OUR TIME

A SOFT, ROLLING PARKLAND WITH GROUPED CLUMPS OF TREES and a few isolated grand specimens is a very English sight. While making the most of natural contours and features, such landscapes also reveal the guidance of human hands: from the eighteenth century, they were both inspired by nature and judiciously enhanced by landscape designers for the enjoyment of landowners. One such parkland, in the eastern part of the county of Cheshire, not far from the old silk-weaving town of Macclesfield, gives the immediate impression of having evolved from an eighteenth-century plan. A long, narrow approach drive brings the visitor past a lake on the one side, and then into an area of mature trees. As the visitor emerges from the trees, a classical, domed and porticoed house suddenly appears up ahead: dream-like, crafted, serene.

There is, in that moment, a grand illusion at work: the house to which the rolling landscape leads did not exist until 1986–87. It was inspired by the vision of ancient Rome captured in villas by the sixteenth-century Venetian architect Andrea Palladio, and those grand British houses that took their cue from his example. It seems at first like a beguiling folly, but within its sublime and jewel-like form is a comfortable home, its intimate connection to its landscape continually reaffirmed through large windows that look out on to the park.

I came here first in 2001, as Architectural Editor of *Country Life*, after a surprise invitation from the owner to see the house. Delivered by taxi from the station, I was taken on a tour by Sebastian de Ferranti, and we enjoyed a convivial lunch in the marble-floored entrance hall. It was a sunlit day, and it was impossible not to be enchanted by the house and the touching pleasure the owner-patron took in his highly individual creation. He enjoyed it all, and it was difficult not to enjoy it in his company.

OPPOSITE An avenue of lime trees leads through the park to the Hall.

FOLLOWING PAGES Henbury Hall from the south, seen across the historic parkland.

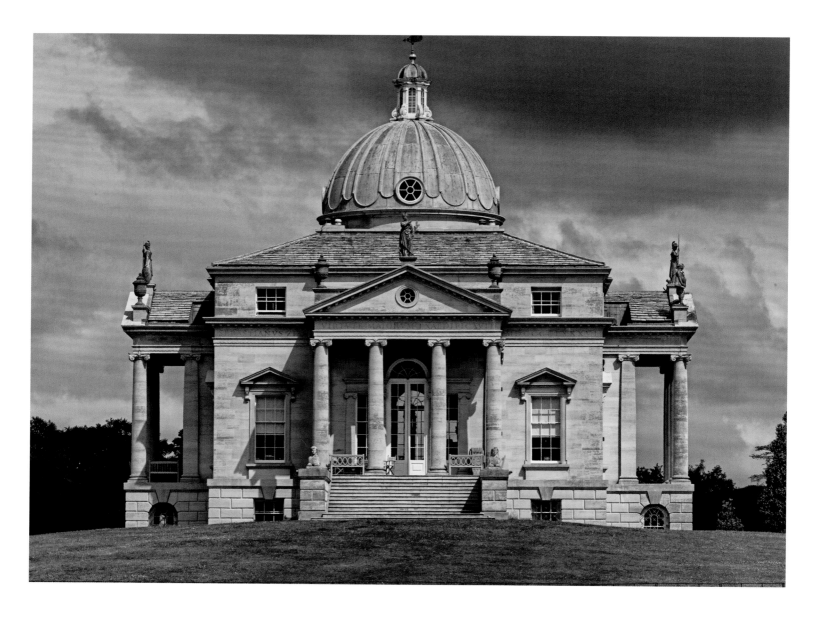

For someone interested in the living country house tradition, and the various permutations of the post-war classical revival, it was a pleasure to write about then – as it is now, nearly twenty years later, at greater length. It is a privilege now to be asked to craft a narrative about the evolution of the house and to be, in a sense, its official biographer. If anything, the house appeals to me more today, as I appreciate the care, love and investment that went into its creation, and am touched by the affection in which it is held by the architect who designed it, and the talented craftsmen and artists who contributed to it. It is a great deal more than the sum of its parts.

The first sight of the house gives the viewer another slight jolt of uncertainty: what is the scale of the building? Is it huge, as the architecture implies? Or is it small? The view reveals more as you take the turn; there is a neighbouring building, of late seventeenth-century origins, which gives a clearer sense of the actual scale. But it is interesting to reflect on how the careful proportions which mark the new house out – and which will be discussed later – could have worked on a different scale.

The eye takes in the pale, warm stone, the rustication of the raised basement level (which would have been known as 'the rustic' in the eighteenth century), the tall windows of the first floor (*piano nobile*), the pediments of the porticoes, the classical figures, the carved Latin inscription, the lead-clad dome, the painted timber lantern. It is a picture, a highly crafted work of art, and a house beloved of its inhabitants – a living thing.

From the first encounter through to the layered interior, the house projects a pleasure in order, and a celebration of the ordered pleasures of a civilised life. It is a homage to both the sixteenth-century villas of the Veneto and to the Anglo-Palladian houses of the eighteenth century – the latter of which were, and still are, associated with traditions of hospitality and country sports.

When a new visitor first discovers that the house was completed in 1987, there is often a sense of surprise that such houses were still being designed at that time. But, as we will discover, the story of this particular house is both nuanced and complex. Sebastian de Ferranti, businessman and land-owner, first explored the idea of commissioning a Modernist house for the site, to be designed by the American-Japanese architect Minoru Yamasaki, but ultimately rejected those designs as just not being appropriate to the historic landscape. And the house we see today is an expression of many things, including the very personal vision of its patron.

Sebastian de Ferranti's father, Sir Vincent, acquired the estate in 1957. He found that the existing house – mostly late seventeenth century, but reduced and remodelled in the eighteenth and the mid-nineteenth centuries – was in desperately poor condition (riddled with dry rot), and so he had it demolished with the intention of building anew. In the meantime, he made the family comfortable in the late seventeenth-century stable and service building, known as the Tenants' Hall, which was adapted for them by architect Harry Fairhurst of Manchester. Sir Vincent and Lady de Ferranti found that their favourite room was the glazed-in carriage arch, it being the only ground-floor room to give a good view of the surrounding park.

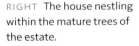

RIGHT The house nestling within the mature trees of the estate.

The 1981 design for the house began as a splendid neo-Romantic painting by Felix Kelly – inspired by Palladio's La Rotonda and Vanbrugh's Temple of the Four Winds.

With the bald site of the former house – and all its potential for wonderful views – still visible, Sebastian de Ferranti had long wanted to build something there. He began with an idea for something more akin to a banqueting house, exploring first Modernist, then Postmodern, then finally unashamedly classical solutions. The key to understanding the house as we see it today is the initial visualisation, in the form of a highly finished oil painting by Felix Kelly, painter, set designer and adviser on houses to a number of people, including – as a result of the Henbury project – HRH The Prince of Wales at Highgrove.

Kelly's essentially neo-Romantic vision was inspired by Palladio's famous 1570s La Rotonda (also known as Villa Capra) and by Sir John Vanbrugh's reworking of Palladio as expressed by his 1720s domed park building at Castle Howard, Yorkshire, which came to be known as the Temple of the Four Winds. Kelly's painting of this was intended as the expression of the design he explored with Sebastian de Ferranti, and it became the reference point for its actual design development.

Plans for the house were then taken forward by Quinlan Terry, one of the leading modern classical architects, who prepared a full set of drawings and secured planning permission. But Sebastian de Ferranti wished to develop the design more in the spirit of Kelly's painting. He parted company with Terry and appointed – on the suggestion of George Howard of Castle Howard, and Felix Kelly – Julian Bicknell, who took the design to a final approved version. Bicknell helped Sebastian de Ferranti to realise what some of his family and friends must have thought was an impossible dream: a modern Palladian-inspired country house and a late twentieth-century expression of Palladio's La Rotonda.

The voluminous correspondence still preserved at the house in 2018 reflects Sebastian de Ferranti's intense personal involvement and interest in delivering the detail of the design, expressed in sketches and discussion with Kelly and others. Sebastian de Ferranti died in 2015, but this book has drawn on personal family archives while providing a chance to interview Julian Bicknell on site, as well as the interior designer, David Mlinaric, craftsmen who worked on the project, including Dick Reid and Paul Czainski, artists including Hazel Morgan and many of Sebastian de Ferranti's friends.

LEFT Simon Verity's sculpture of Diana, originally commissioned for the south portico of the Hall and relocated to the lakeside.

David Mlinaric, who became involved at the time the house was still being built, remembers vividly the sheer fun of working with Sebastian de Ferranti. The fullness and confidence of the decorative and furnishing schemes contrived by Mlinaric is reflected in how little has changed between 1986–7 and 2018, save for some additional gilding within the principal reception rooms, especially in the dining room.

There were the inevitable problems in construction: bad weather slowed the delivery of stone, the execution of the building was complex and required rigorous onsite management. But the overall result was a source

ABOVE Flowering *Magnolia* x *loebneri* 'Leonard Messel' within the grounds.

of enormous satisfaction to Sebastian, and he is remembered as having kept photographs in his pocket to show acquaintances, as a proud parent might show off a new infant.

This book is intended to record the story of one mid-1980s house. However, it also casts its net wider, to explore the history of the estate, of the Palladian and Palladian-inspired houses that provided the model, of the different stages of design and building, and of the personality of the patron. Sebastian de Ferranti was a complex, energetic, but always courteous, figure, who jokingly referred in letters to his 'Latin' temperament. He was especially proud of both his Venetian ancestry and his inventor grandfather and namesake, who introduced the first alternating current electrical power plant to the United Kingdom.

RIGHT At the heart of the *piano nobile*: from the central great hall looking into the drawing room.

A HOUSE IN OUR TIME

Alongside a high-flying career in business and manufacture, Sebastian de Ferranti should be recognised as a distinct form of late twentieth-century country gentleman. A public-spirited figure, a trustee of the Tate and on the board of the Hallé, he was keen on skiing, fox hunting and polo, and, later, carriage driving. These latter pleasures he shared with a circle of friends including HRH Prince Philip, Duke of Edinburgh, a regular visitor to Henbury. There is a polo ground at Henbury, the house providing a delightful backdrop to the games and prize-givings. Sebastian de Ferranti's passion for classical architecture was also shared by HRH The Prince of Wales.

The interest of Henbury Hall as a signifier of the classical revival should not be underestimated; John Martin Robinson included the house as a 'triumphant' postscript to his book *The Latest Country Houses* (1984), writing: 'In many ways the design of Henbury marks the culmination of the architectural trends studied in this book, combining as it does the romantic vision of the amateurs inspired by the English eighteenth century, and the recent scholarly revival of Palladianism as the style best suited to the design of a "gentleman's house" in the late twentieth century ... [Sebastian de Ferranti] looked over most of the world for a Modern house that would provide a suitable model for Henbury, but found nothing which gave him the particular excitement he derived from the villas of Palladio. This, combined with the visual demands of the English park setting, more or less dictated a Classical house.'

John Martin Robinson's book was a revelation to an audience eagerly interested in country life and country houses. Most orthodox Modernists, educated in architectural schools that see no value in the continuing interpretations of classical style, turn their faces away from tradition. But new classical country houses have remained a major feature of the country house world – as evidenced by the regular appearance of such houses in the pages of *Country Life*.

Looking back to the 1980s, when the country was moving out of the political turmoil of the previous decade, it seems that Henbury Hall may indeed have marked a new moment of confidence in the world of traditional architecture in a technological age, and of the country house, in the UK and elsewhere. After a visit, Lord Gibson (a chairman of the National Trust) wrote that Sebastian de Ferranti was of the 'Shirley class', referring to Sir Robert Shirley, who built an elegant church and was remembered for 'doing the best of things in the worst of times'.

Thirty-five years on, the house remains an admired achievement of the age. It is an extraordinary house that occupies an unusual position in the story of twentieth-century British architecture. It rises like a dream from verdant historic parkland, commanding yet comfortable; modern but sourced from historical and international references. No 'pre-knowledge' of these is necessary to enjoy its simple, sculpted elegance and the harmony of its proportions. The comfort and style of its interiors can be casually enjoyed by the family, or expanded to suit a house party, with an extra-long table down the centre of the Palladian hall, and all the bedrooms of the house and the Tenants' Hall wing filled to capacity.

The new Henbury Hall was built on the site of the older house which Sir Vincent de Ferranti had had pulled down. When Sebastian de Ferranti died

OPPOSITE A very English vista: the ride running south from the house.

in 2015, his obituarist in the *Daily Telegraph* celebrated the new Henbury Hall as 'one of Britain's finest twentieth-century country houses' and noted that it was inspired by the work of Andrea Palladio, the sixteenth-century Venetian architect whose designs and treatise on architecture – *I quattro libri* – were the inspiration for so many of the finest British country houses in the eighteenth century.

The result of the Henbury Hall commission was a triumph. The shell was completed in 1986, with interiors and furnishing completed the following year. It had a determined patron who wanted the best of everything, and an imaginative architect with a vision of the adaptability of the classical tradition.

Subtle alterations to the earlier models were evolved to create a house of refinement and convenience. The internal plan of the house, the proportions and the details, although drawn from Renaissance Italian and English eighteenth-century models, were adapted to contemporary patterns of use and life. On the 'rustic' level is the low-ceilinged entrance hall, oval in the centre – a dignified reception hall – with service rooms around it, including kitchen, laundry, nursery and cloakroom, as well as a convenient breakfast room.

A tightly composed cantilevered stair rises up from the oval hall on the north-west side, the eye drawn up to its suitably Piranesian form, reaching the second storey. The arrival at the *piano nobile* is unforgettable, as the stair leads you into a huge tripartite central hall which connects with the interior of the dome. There is a large drawing room and a dining room, with a smaller sitting room (morning room) and study (library) in the south-east and south-west corners respectively.

All the rooms on this floor are 5.4 metres (18 feet) high and embellished with elaborate cornices and elegantly carved door cases. On the second storey are four bedrooms with attached bathrooms and dressing rooms, two of which can double as single rooms (several of the spaces are ingeniously contrived within the volume of the portico roofs). These rooms are approached from a second-floor gallery which looks down into the great hall. The northern corners of the *piano nobile* contain respectively the staircase and a passenger and food lift, as well as a butler's pantry.

Remarkably, it seems only four houses in eighteenth-century England were built on something like the model of La Rotonda (and two of these also drew on other significant precedents). Two of them were demolished earlier in the twentieth century, and only one other country house has been designed in this spirit since the mid-1980s. Henbury Hall represents the revival of an estate and the vibrant realisation of one man's dream, working with a creative team and a confident, inventive architect. It has certainly added a chapter to the story of the classical house in Britain, and the long and fertile reach of Palladio's Roman-inspired architecture.

The stories of remarkable houses are so much more than the story of plans and estimates, designers and planners; they happen because of very personal decisions, and are always a collaboration. Sebastian de Ferranti wrote a letter to a niece in 1998, over ten years after the work was completed, which summarised the project: 'My father pulled down the house at Henbury ... It was his intention to rebuild, but as he was then coming up to seventy he felt he didn't have the energy. The site therefore remained empty for about forty years.'

ABOVE AND OPPOSITE
Henbury Hall seen at
twilight and at night.

He conceded that his first inclination 'was to build a modern house, and
to this end I talked to Mr Yamasaki, who interpreted Gothic design in a
modern idiom … I liked his approach. However, when it came to a modern
building set in a wet green Cheshire park, it did not look well.'

His letter continued by introducing his own, very clear account of the
design process: 'Felix Kelly, who was a New Zealander, and had painted
a series of houses in America and England, consistently produced beautiful buildings. I had known him for some time, so together we looked at
various buildings. And came to the conclusion that a variation on Palladio's
ideas appealed to me the most.'

Intriguingly, Sebastian de Ferranti hinted at a broader ambition, to
stimulate interest in good design through this personal project: 'It is my
view that the modern architects who are no longer taught perspective or
figurative drawing are not a suitable profession to produce a regular,
aesthetically pleasing house.'

From this point onwards, the narrative was simple, if not entirely
straightforward: 'Felix Kelly did a series of drawings and paintings, which
we worked up into a final view, and I then asked Quinlan Terry to produce
some plans. He was Erith's partner and was a very likeable man.'

Terry's preliminary designs were used to achieve planning permission
and building regulations, but in the long run, Sebastian de Ferranti decided
he did not want to continue with Terry: 'In talking to George Howard at

A HOUSE IN OUR TIME

Castle Howard, he suggested Julian Bicknell, who had worked with Kelly at Castle Howard, and it was he who produced the plan, based on Felix's drawings.'

De Ferranti thought Bicknell had 'great skills and knowledge of classical architecture' but was not familiar with the requirements of gentlemen's residences 'such as butler's pantries and linen cupboards'. However, he found him 'an agreeable man to work with', and other specialists on the project recall the importance of Bicknell's adaptability and charm.

De Ferranti's letter observed: 'It is a very small house compared with the Rotonda at Vicenza, Mereworth Castle in Kent, or Foot's Cray and Nuthall Temple, all of which are square, domed, portico houses. All these have six columns. For economy, and because of the size, there are four columns to each portico at Henbury.'

He signed off his letter with an anecdote which will introduce the exploration that comes in the pages which follow: 'When the late Lord Derby saw it, he said what a magnificent lodge it was, but asked where was the main house?' It was a story he liked to repeat, one that sums up some of the particular charm of this 'palace in miniature'.

FOLLOWING PAGES
The house from the west, the fully realised dream of manufacturer and entrepreneur Sebastian de Ferranti.

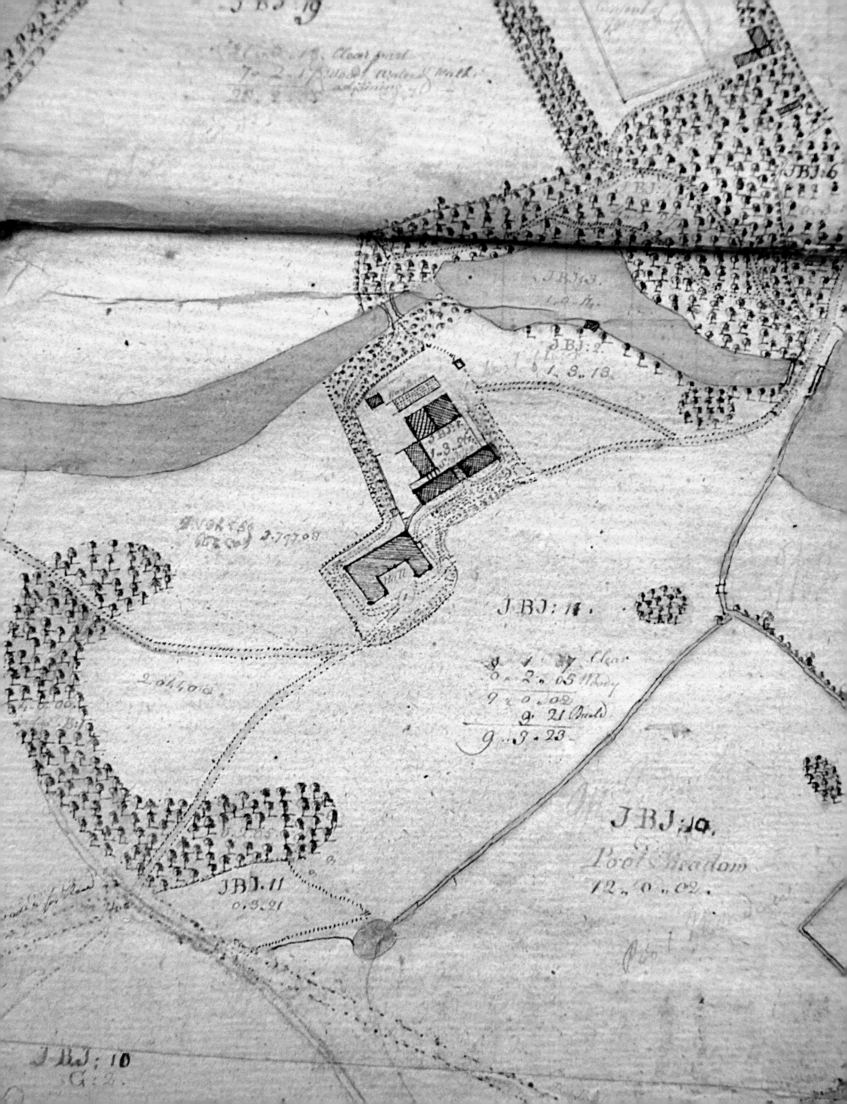

CHAPTER II
A COUNTRY ESTATE

PART OF THE PARTICULAR RESONANCE OF HENBURY HALL IS derived from its place within the history of the landscape, taking its part in a long, patchworked procession of habitation and occupation. The story of the estate's ownership is a typical dynastic puzzle of tactical landholdings, family alliances, public office holders – including MPs, High Sheriffs and Lord Lieutenants – alongside mill owners and bankers aspiring to become landed gentry.

Henbury was part of the ancient Prestbury parish, which appears to have been settled in Saxon times, and is today renowned for its Norman chapel. The Henbury estate was sold by the Trussell family, in 1350, to John de Davenport of the manor of Weltrough, in whose family it descended until the seventeenth century. A 1558 description of the estate alludes to a house of several courts of buildings, including stables, barns, turf houses, hay houses, ox houses, cow houses and a dove house. There was a deer park – a clear sign of the status of the landowner – as well as fishponds, orchards and a hop yard.

The history is not crystal clear, and there may only have been a hunting lodge on the site of the current Henbury Hall itself. But an account from 1640, published in the *Cheshire Sheaf*, is believed to describe a house associated with the Henbury estate, and details 'a very sumptuous house with courts, gardens, orchards well stocked with good fruits, dove house, banqueting hall, excellent stables and other outhouses fair and convenient, the building of which cost nearly £5,000'.

In 1656, sole heiress Isabella Davenport married the exotically named Sir Fulk Lucy of Charlecote in Warwickshire, great-grandson of the Sir Thomas Lucy who reputedly tried the young William Shakespeare for

OPPOSITE A map of the Henbury estate in 1794, showing the impressive extent of the eighteenth-century house.

poaching. Sir Fulk was knighted in 1661, elected MP for Cheshire in 1664, and was a captain in Lord Gerard's First Troop of Horse Guards in 1666–7. He was a canny operator in Parliament; Sir Richard Wiseman called him 'touchily and peevishly angry … [he] watcheth who bids most for him.' After his death in 1677, the estate passed to his eldest son, and then to his second son, George, who sold it in 1693. It is interesting to note that seventeenth-century documents refer to the park without mentioning a mansion house, one from 1675 calling it 'all that parke or in poles grounds comonly known by the name of Henbury parke' and another, from 1687, 'All that Parke or impaled ground comonly called or knowne by the name of Henbury Parke'.

The first mansion house certain to have been located on the site of the current Henbury Hall seems to have been built between 1687 and 1693. It is documented in a conveyance in the Cheshire Record Office that refers to the 'Mansion House called or known by the name of Henbury-house in Henbury'. Sir William Meredith, 2nd Baronet, son of a famous cavalry officer, acquired the Henbury estate in 1693 and took up residency in 1698. It seems likely that it was during this five-year hiatus that he constructed a new classical house, over extensive brick cellarage. Some mullioned windows in the former stables (later converted into the Tenants' Hall and then into a house in 1957) are of a late seventeenth-century type.

RIGHT AND FAR RIGHT Surviving late seventeenth-century elements: the roof and the exterior of the rear of the stable block; and the cellars of the old house.

BELOW RIGHT Seen from the lower lake, the barns and stables of the old house form a rambling, village-like complex.

FOLLOWING PAGES The late seventeenth-century roof structure of the entrance to the old stable yard.

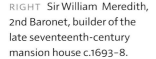

RIGHT Sir William Meredith, 2nd Baronet, builder of the late seventeenth-century mansion house c.1693–8.

Others are nineteenth-century copies. Although stuccoed by the nineteenth century, it is likely that the house was originally brick with stone dressings, as were the stables.

Sir William also seems to have been active in landscaping, creating the upper lake around 1717. A 'Survey by Matthias Aston, Anno 1727' gives a 'Mapp of the Manour of Henbury' with the upper lake and a small round pond in the position of the lower lake. A 1794 map gives a clearer indication of the house of the eighteenth century, showing a U-shaped courtyard plan entered from the south, in the middle of the courtyard. There is a story that Meredith reduced the house substantially because 'he arrived from one of his foreign travels a day or two earlier than expected and found his staff merrymaking in the Hall. He was livid with anger and ordered the wing of the house to be pulled down.' However, it seems more likely that this downsizing occurred much later, in the mid-nineteenth century.

The 3rd Baronet, also Sir William, succeeded his grandfather in 1752 and was Tory M P for Wigan and a Lord of the Admiralty under the influence of Lord Rockingham. Walpole called him 'a convert from Jacobitism; inflexibly serious, and of no clear head; yet practice formed him to a manner of speaking that had weight and was worth attending to by those who had patience for it.' His father, Amos, was depicted in a famous group of portraits at Tabley Hall showing Cheshire gentlemen who met in 1715, at the time of the Jacobite rising, to resolve which faction they would follow (they opted to defend George I).

Despite being a mayor of Macclesfield, privy councillor and comptroller of the household, and despite having 'at considerable risk to his own person' saved the life of prime minister Lord North from the mob, the

3rd Baronet died in obscurity, in Lyons, in 1790. One of his sisters became Viscountess Curzon and another was Countess Ferrers but, as the baronet had no children, the title died with him. After spending beyond his means, he had sold Henbury estate eleven years before his death.

John Bower Jodrell acquired Henbury in 1779 for £24,000. Either he or his son, Francis Bower Jodrell, may have remodelled the house, but their name is best remembered for an outlying piece of their Cheshire property, Jodrell Bank, which became the base for radar research in the mid-twentieth century. There has been a tradition that Humphry Repton may have been involved in the landscaping at Henbury in this period (he worked for a number of Cheshire landowners between 1790 and 1802), but there is no documentary evidence.

In 1835, John Charles Ryle, banker and MP, bought the Henbury estate for £54,000. His family had a long association with textiles and dyeing, being major silk manufacturers in Macclesfield. The house appears to have retained the courtyard U-shape: an 1830 map seems to indicate the original footprint, with the stable ranges to the right.

An 1820 inventory lists all the rooms of the then house, with Library, Passages & Landing Stairs, Front Entrance, Drawing Room, Breakfast Room, Dining Room and Study. The bedrooms included the Velvet Bed Room, Canopy Bed Room, Blue Moreen Bed Room, Red Print Bed Room, Grey Bed Room, White Bed Room; as well as Nursery & School Room and Nursery Bedroom and a Lower Bed Room. The domestic offices included Butler's Bed Room, Pantry Bed Room, Butler's Pantry, China Closset, Servants' Hall, Servants' Brushing Room, Larder, Pantry, Lobby Kitchen, Scullery, Laundry, Wash House, Boot Room, Small Cellar, House Keeper's Cellar, First Beer Cellar, Second Beer Cellar, Ale Cellar, Brew House, Dairy Houses.

A strong flavour of the social cachet of a country estate is given in the memoirs of John Charles's son, the second John Charles Ryle (later the

BELOW LEFT John Charles Ryle, Macclesfield banker and MP, who bought the estate in 1835. His son's memoirs include an atmospheric account of life at the house and in the surrounding country estates.

BELOW RIGHT Pale Lodge, the main lodge, built in the nineteenth century in the Old English style, with characteristic Cheshire half-timbering.

first Anglican Bishop of Liverpool), as he recalled the move to Henbury
from Park House in Macclesfield: 'Park House, though an agreeable place
in itself, was far too near a growing manufacturing town, and we really had
no society of what could be called real gentlemen and ladies. Henbury on
the contrary was thoroughly in the country, was in itself a very pleasant
place, and was surrounded by the residences of gentlemen. Standing outside the door at Henbury on any fine evening, we could hear the dinner bell
ring at Mr Hibbert's of Birtles, at Mr Thornycroft's of Thornycroft, at Mr
Davenport's of Capesthorne. Harehill, Alderley Park, Astle and Joddrell
[sic] Hall were also all within an easy distance.'

In 1842, after his father's sudden bankruptcy, the estate was sold.
Writing some thirty-two years later, Ryle said the memories were as vivid
as if they were yesterday, and recalled how 'men-servants, butler, under
butler, footman, coachman, groom, housekeeper, housemaids, in fact a
whole staff, one of whom had been with us for 30 years, another 25, two
more 20 ... were all at once dismissed, and paid off.' They left in August,
when 'the place was in full beauty in Midsummer but everything seemed
as deserted and silent as a tomb. Morning, noon, and night, the crushing
feeling was upon me, that we were about to leave the place and never come
back again.'

The estate was then bought by Thomas Marsland, MP for Stockport.
In 1850 there is a description in *Bagshaw's Directory* of 'a handsome stuccoed mansion, which opens into a park beautifully wooded, and pleasingly
diversified with gentle undulations. It is now the seat and property of
Major Thomas Marsland.' The 1882 *History of the County Palatine and City of*

ABOVE In front of the house, a family group celebrating the twenty-first birthday of Walter Argyll Brocklehurst in 1901.

Chester says that: 'Major Marsland reduced its size by many rooms' and the Ordnance Survey map of 1872 shows a new footprint with no courtyard to the south, a new kitchen wing to the north, and the main entrance and carriage sweep moved to the east side.

Thomas died in 1854, and was succeeded by his son Edward Marsland (d.1867). Edward's widow, Jane, was in possession of the estate on the night of 18 June 1872, when there was a ten-hour rainstorm. The *Macclesfield Courier* reported that, 'The upper pool to the rear of the carriage drive on the approach to the Hall was swollen to an unprecedented extent by the heavy rain. We have been informed that the water was fourteen feet higher in the pool than has been known on any other occasion.'

Worse was to come, as 'the extraordinary pressure on the embankment forming the carriage road and upon the bridge which ran under it caused them to give way, and the angry waters, freed from their ordinary limits, then commenced a course of havoc and devastation which can be traced as far as the Capesthorne bridge on the Congleton Road.' The county council sued Mrs Marsland for £4,000 for the loss and replacement of bridges; she challenged the suit and finally, in 1875, a ruling was given which established the principle of 'act of God' (and the legal requirement that all dams over a certain size should be vetted by a specialist 'Panel Engineer'). However, fearing bankruptcy, Mrs Marsland had sold up in 1874.

The estate was then purchased by a local silk manufacturer, Thomas Unett Brocklehurst, for £9,000. In nearby Macclesfield, three successive John Brocklehursts had been important figures in the silk industry's expansion, one joining Acton and Street button manufacturers in 1748 and

ABOVE LEFT Pony and trap in front of the Tenants' Hall, early twentieth century.

BELOW LEFT The interior of the Tenants' Hall decked out for an estate entertainment.

ABOVE RIGHT The waterfall in the gardens in the early twentieth century

becoming a partner in 1759; his son followed him, and steered the company, by then Joseph Street & Co, into silk manufacture. The third John formed a partnership with his brother Thomas, and the firm was known as J. & T. Brocklehurst: the family's story is told in Mary Crozier's *An Old Silk Family, 1745–1945* (1947). John Brocklehurst was elected one of the two MPs for Macclesfield in 1832.

It is not clear whether Thomas Unett, acquiring the property after the flood, had to repair the lakes, walks and entrance viaduct – the house, on high ground, had not been damaged, nor had the stables and barns. The third lake, which linked to the Big Wood, was not reinstated, and nor was its stone dam (the stones of which can still be found scattered in Big Wood). Brocklehurst employed Mr Aspinall of Macclesfield to renovate the two remaining pools at Henbury at the huge cost of £6,000.

As well as acquiring many plants from abroad (and an enormous Japanese temple bell for the garden – see page 193), Brocklehurst was also responsible for some remodelling of the stables, where there is a date stone of 1884 with his coat of arms. Part of the ground floor became the 'Tenants' Hall', where tenants could be entertained on Lady Day, when they paid their annual rents, a tradition that continued into the 1960s.

RIGHT View of old
Henbury Hall which
shows the curved
service range to the
right, linking the house
to the Tenants' Hall.

The Brocklehursts also made some alterations to the house and occupied it fully. Inventories indicate that the house remained a substantial country house, with numerous rooms dedicated to the residential domestic servants, but the drop in the number of rooms, from sixty-five in the 1820 inventory to fifty-seven in 1918, shows clearly that the house had shrunk in size.

RIGHT A plan showing
the relationship of
the three lakes before
the flood of 1872 (the
lowest lake was never
re-created).

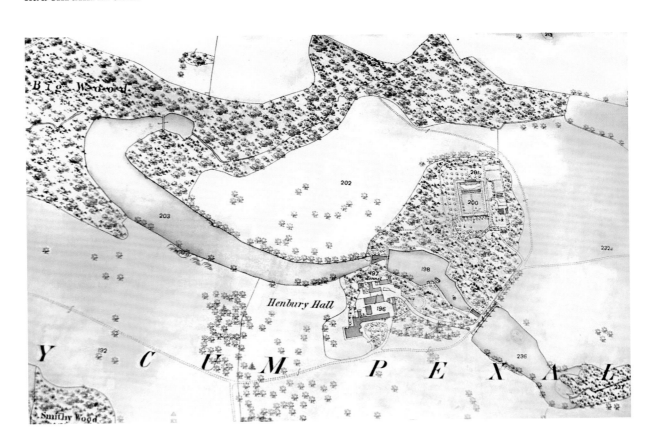

ABOVE The house seen from the south-west shortly before demolition; originally red brick with stone dressings, in the nineteenth century the elevations were rendered to appear like stone.

BELOW LEFT The house from the north-west, showing the effect of some of the mid-nineteenth-century alterations that had drastically reduced the house in size and also left the north elevation an eccentric composition.

BELOW RIGHT The derelict state of the interiors was recorded just before the house was demolished in 1957.

RIGHT A detail of one of the internal door cases, probably mid-eighteenth century in date.

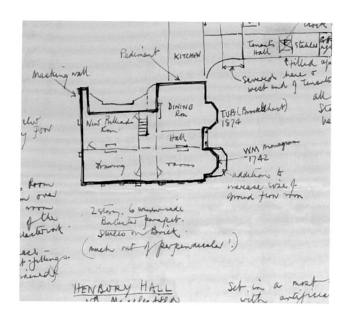

Having been twice mayor of Macclesfield and a lieutenant colonel of the 5th Hussars, Brocklehurst died in 1886 at the age of sixty-three. Like other owners of Henbury Hall before him, he had also served as High Sheriff of the county, in 1866–67. The estate passed, in 1926, to Edward Brocklehurst after he inherited from a cousin who died young. A solicitor and JP, Edward Brocklehurst occupied the house until he died in 1957.

Photographs of the house taken in 1957 show a Victorianised interior with some rooms retaining 'decent mid-C18 rococo plasterwork', as John Martin Robinson described it in *A Guide to the Country Houses of the North-West*. The sale catalogue listed the principal rooms of reception: 'Drawing room, dining room, billiard room, garden room, vestibule and main hall, principal staircase and landing. Also smoking room, ante room and cloak-room. Nursery and five bedrooms.' Plus 'old billiards room'. It also noted the 'Jacobean, Georgian and Early Victorian period furniture [and] choice pieces of walnut marquetry'.

When Sir Vincent de Ferranti bought the Henbury Hall estate in 1957, he had intended to live in the substantial main house at the centre of the estate. In the photographs, it looks stately enough: two storeys, six bays, giant order pilasters, and one bay in from both ends the tall ground-floor windows (then French doors) have semicircular pediments. On the north-east corner, a lower curved range links the service end to the Tenants' Hall and stables. The Hall was sited on raised land, with excellent views of the park; the main pedimented entrance to the east was set between two three-storey canted bays, which formed the effect of two towers.

However, the house was also apparently 'riddled with dry rot'. According to Harry Fairhurst, the Manchester-based architect who converted the Tenants' Hall and stables into a house for Sir Vincent and Lady de Ferranti from 1957, the last resident member of the Brocklehurst family is reputed to have been sitting in his armchair in the drawing room when the floor collapsed under him. The old Hall, the home of the Lucys, Merediths, Marslands and Brocklehursts, was, like so many country houses which in these years seemed doomed relics of an earlier age, pulled down, leaving just the solid brick, vaulted, mostly late seventeenth-century cellars below the ground.

CHAPTER III
FERRANTIS

GRAND HOUSES DO NOT GET BUILT WITHOUT MONEY, AND MANY of Palladio's patrons were entrepreneurial merchant princes. The money that enabled the building of Henbury Hall came from the Ferranti family firm – known as 'Ferranti's' – founded by Sebastian Ziani de Ferranti in the 1880s. He was a gifted inventor and instinctive innovator; after his death, the family firm's chairmanship passed to his son, Sir Vincent de Ferranti, and then to grandsons, first Sebastian and then Basil.

Ziani de Ferranti's Italian family roots can be traced back to eighth-century Venice and included such figures as Doge Sebastiano Ziani in the 1170s, famed as one of the great planners of the city. Sebastian Ziani de Ferranti himself was born in 1864, on Bold Street in Liverpool at the home of his British grandfather, a successful portrait painter called William Scott. His mother, Juliana, was a talented concert pianist. She had had a family of three daughters and two sons with her first husband, Stanislas Szczepanowski, a Polish guitarist and revolutionary, when she met her second husband, Giulio Cesare Ziani de Ferranti, at a concert in Ostend. He was an Italian portrait photographer who went on to set up a photography studio in Liverpool with her painter father.

Cesare's own father was a much-travelled classical guitarist and composer called Marco Aurelio Ziani de Ferranti, who became guitarist to the court of King Leopold of Belgium. So Ziani de Ferranti grew up in a family with a deep musical heritage – from his mother and her first husband, from his father's father, and from his mother's sister Emily, through her marriage to Charles Seymour, lead violinist of the Hallé orchestra. However, his early talents were as a draughtsman and artist (an exquisite picture of a steam engine, which he painted when he was eleven years old, hangs still

OPPOSITE The framed painting of a steam engine by the young Sebastian Ziani de Ferranti (1864–1930), aged eleven; one of the early manifestations of his inventive mind. The large portrait below the painting of the train is of Sebastian Ziani de Ferranti's mother, Madame Juliana Ziani de Ferranti, painted by her father, William Scott.

Illustrious
ancestor: Sebastiano Ziani,
Doge of Venice, with the
Pope, after the Battle of
Salvore, painted by Jacopo
Bassano, 1590–94.

at Henbury Hall) and inventor. By the age of fourteen, he had begun to develop the idea for a dynamo that was to become his first commercial invention.

At Hampstead School and then at the Benedictine-run St Augustine's College in Ramsgate, Ziani de Ferranti took an interest in science. In 1880, he enrolled to study engineering at University College, London, but his father fell ill soon after. By 1881 he was obliged to leave and find work to support his family. He became a laboratory assistant for the Chief Research Engineer at electrical engineers Siemens, based in Charlton in London. Historian J. F. Wilson says that this 'dark, handsome young man with flashing bright eyes and excited oratory' instilled confidence in others. He was also a man who during his working life took enormous commercial

RIGHT Marco Aurelio
Ziani de Ferranti
(1801–1878), classical
guitarist and composer,
grandfather of the
inventor Sebastian Ziani
de Ferranti.

FAR RIGHT Giulio
Cesare Ziani de Ferranti
(1831–1902), known as
Cesare, son of Marco
Aurelio and father of the
inventor..

risks, always driven by technological innovation and curiosity. Within a
few years he would establish a worldwide reputation as a leading advocate
of high-tension alternating-current (AC) generation and distribution, and
during the course of his career, he was to take out some 176 patents.

While still at Siemens, he worked on an idea for the armature of alter-
nators with Francis Thompson (a family friend who, like his father, was a
photographer) and a solicitor called Francis Ince. In 1882, he set up his first
company: Ferranti, Thompson and Ince. The company began to manufacture the dynamo Ziani de Ferranti had developed as a boy, the prototype
of which was advanced, in association with Sir William Thompson (later
Lord Kelvin), as the Ferranti-Thompson alternator. Although this first
company was wound up after a year, in 1885 a new firm was launched: S. Z.
de Ferranti. The partners were Francis Ince, again, and Charles Sparks.
Ziani de Ferranti married Ince's daughter Gertrude in 1888. She is remembered as a formidable matriarch at the head of her family of seven children.

Ziani de Ferranti's next break occurred at the heart of Aesthetic Movement London. Sir Coutts Lindsay's Grosvenor Gallery championed artists
such as Leighton, Burne-Jones and Albert Moore and was associated
with pallid young aesthetes – of a type celebrated in a line in Gilbert
and Sullivan's *Patience* as a 'greenery-yallery, Grosvenor Gallery foot-in-
the-grave young man'.

The gallery was concerned with both selling art and entertaining cus-
tomers – and was the first London gallery to be lit by electricity. This was
installed on the advice of the 26th Earl of Crawford, who had seen it used
in the Paris Exhibition of 1882. Blanche, the wife of Coutts Lindsay, was a
Rothschild and able to fund such novelties. Ziani de Ferranti sold the gallery an alternator in 1885, and in 1886 was appointed company engineer,
with a brief to expand the electricity supply to the gallery's neighbours.

This enterprise proved to be a creative spark. By way of the Grosvenor
Gallery Electricity Supply Corporation, a new company was formed – the
London Electrical Supply Corporation (LESCO) – set up in 1887 by Sir
Coutts and his brother-in-law Lord Wantage, with Ziani de Ferranti as chief
engineer. The company raised funding to build Deptford Power Station,
entirely designed by Ziani de Ferranti and, at the time, the largest power

RIGHT The inventor
Sebastian Ziani de
Ferranti (1864–1930).

FAR RIGHT Gertrude
Ziani de Ferranti (1869–
1959), wife of Sebastian
Ziani de Ferranti, with
whom she had seven
children.

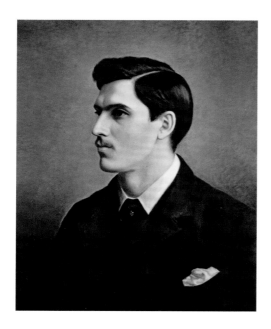

station in the world. The press dubbed Ziani de Ferranti the 'Michelangelo of Deptford'; the power produced by the station – intended to light two million lamps – required a distribution pressure of 10,000 volts along cables and transformers, challenging the most advanced electric-current engineering of the day. The monumental station opened in 1890 and, while it was hugely admired – and is considered by historians as the pioneer of modern electricity substations – it was not a commercial success.

Ziani de Ferranti moved on to other projects. The business had been refounded in 1888 as a limited company, S.Z. de Ferranti Ltd. From 1894, they provided street lighting in Portsmouth and, during this process, the company introduced rectifiers that converted alternating current to the direct current required for 'arc' lamps. In 1896, S. Z. de Ferranti Ltd

RIGHT Sebastian Ziani
de Ferranti (centre back
in the doorway, looking
at the camera) and his
family at Baslow Hall,
Derbyshire.

opened a factory in Hollinwood in Oldham producing steam-driven alter-
nators, switchgear and rectifiers, instruments and transformers.

Making a company successful is always a challenge: Ferranti Ltd was
re-created in 1901 but then went into voluntary receivership. It was re-
launched in 1905 under the chairmanship of Andrew Tait. Ziani de Ferranti was asked to focus on invention and innovation, although he succeeded Tait as chairman in 1927. As J. F. Wilson writes, Ferranti was 'an
incorrigible developer of ideas and machines, interfering constantly with
designs as they progressed from the drawing-board into production, and
while this technology-led strategy resulted in striking improvements to
electrical engineering, it also diverted scarce resources.'

The company now focused on manufacturing switchgear, transformers,
meters and other electrical equipment. In 1907, it supplied switchgear
units for the Cunard liners *Mauretania* and *Lusitania*. (The *Lusitania* was
torpedoed by a German submarine in 1915 and sank with the loss of all
1,198 on board; it was this event that finally brought the United States into
the First World War.)

Ziani de Ferranti's instinctive curiosity was unending. In 1909, he spent a holiday in France and visited an aviation exhibition. This inspired him to develop a gyroscopic design to help aircraft achieve greater airborne stability. It was an invention of remarkable foresight and, although it was not put into production at the time, it influenced the company's work on gyroscopic instruments during the Second World War.

From 1912, the firm extended into pioneering domestic appliances such as fires, cookers and irons. During this period, Ziani de Ferranti collaborated with J. & P. Coats Ltd on textile machinery; with Vickers on desuperheating turbines; and with J. Hopkinson & Co. on steam stop-valves. Ziani de Ferranti was a recognised industry leader and established the British Electrical and Allied Manufacturers' Association, of which he became president in 1912. He was the first president of the Institution of Electrical Engineers (IEE) in 1910–12, and was awarded an honorary doctorate by the University of Manchester in 1912.

Ziani de Ferranti's work with J. Hopkinson & Co. gave the family a taste of real wealth and, in 1913, he invested in a country property. This was Baslow Hall in Derbyshire, a house designed in seventeenth-century style but built only in 1907, probably by the architects Weightman & Hadfield. Ziani de Ferranti filled the newly minted house with technology, including the installation of a 25-horsepower oil engine which, until 1923, operated an electrical plant powering every modern labour-saving device, including an electric laundry, a lawnmower and a floodlit tennis court.

However, alongside worldly success there came personal tragedy. Ziani de Ferranti's two elder sons, Basil and Vincent, both served in the First World War and were both awarded the Military Cross. But Major Basil de Ferranti MC was killed in action in July 1917, near Ypres, while serving with the 24th Heavy Artillery Group at Messines. He was buried in the Wimereux Communal Cemetery. The loss must have been shattering.

Like so many companies, the S. Z. de Ferranti works were converted into a munitions factory during the war, in this case under Ziani de Ferranti's direct management. This marked the beginning of a long period of government contracts. After the war, in the 1920s and 1930s,

Baslow Hall

The All Electric House.

With the compliments of Dr. and Mrs. S. Z. de Ferranti.

ABOVE LEFT
The electronic transformer invented by Sebastian Ziani de Ferranti; photograph of 1899.

the company moved into fields such as audio-frequency transformers for radios, and also innovated in the area of domestic appliances, producing water heaters and electric clocks.

When the Central Electricity Generating Board was set up in 1926 to construct a national supply grid, Ferranti successfully secured the commission for the largest single share of orders for three-phase transformers. In recognition of his visionary advocacy of the National Grid, the IEE awarded Ziani de Ferranti the Faraday Medal in 1924. In 1927, he was made a Fellow of the Royal Society.

In 1930, following an operation in Switzerland, Ziani de Ferranti died. He was succeeded by his son Vincent, who had survived the First World War, having volunteered at its outbreak. He served in Gallipoli and the Middle East with the 67th Field Company, the Royal Engineers, with whom he achieved the rank of captain (as well as, like his brother, being awarded the Military Cross). His formal education was confined to Repton School, Derbyshire, but his military history was more than enough evidence that he had the leadership qualities needed to take over the family firm. He married Dorothy Hettie Wilson, daughter of

ABOVE RIGHT
A Ferranti audio transformer, 1920s–30s.

BELOW RIGHT
A Ferranti transformer, 1920s–30s.

Reginald Page Wilson, a consulting engineer, in 1919, and they went on to have two sons and three daughters.

Sir Vincent (he was knighted in 1948) inherited his father's belief in the value of technological innovation. By 1921, he was manager of the transformer department, where he helped establish Ferranti Ltd as Britain's leading firm in the design and production of larger units. Conscious of the 1903 failure of the business, he strove always to maintain a balance between technological and financial priorities. Sir Vincent was chairman until 1963, during which time Ferranti Ltd established itself as one of Britain's leading electronics, avionics and electrical engineering firms.

Its most successful products were power transformers, on-board radar equipment, computers, integrated circuits and numerical control machines. Factories were set up in Wythenshawe, Bracknell and Edinburgh, and innovations included the development of the thermionic valves (or vacuum tubes) used in radios and later in computers. In 1933, the company landed one of its biggest contracts, providing detonation fuses to the British government. In 1935, a new factory was opened in Moston, Manchester, and it was from here, in 1937, that the company began to manufacture televisions, as well as avionic and naval instruments, including gyroscopic equipment for the government.

The Second World War led to a leap in government orders for fuses, as well as involvement in the development of radar (Identification Friend or Foe) Mark 1 and, from 1942, the manufacture of AUK units for the Royal Navy (these were the 'eye' of the ship's radar systems). A Scottish factory was opened in 1943 to make gyro gun sights (GGS) for fighter aircraft. Vincent de Ferranti's knighthood in 1948 was in recognition of his firm's contribution to the war effort, an honour he publicly dedicated to the thousands of Ferranti's employees.

After the war, a new factory, Avenue Works, built large-scale power transformers on the Oldham Hollinwood site. It was a period of expansion not only in military hardware – with a new guided missile for the British government (later known as 'Bloodhound') – but also in the field of computer technology. In 1951, Ferranti Ltd was the first company to produce, in its factory at Moston, a commercially available version of the Mark I computer, the first step in the technological transformation of domestic life and the social media revolution which followed.

Ferranti's continued to be at the forefront of innovation as one of the first manufacturers to use silicon as a semi-conducting material. It was also the first European company to make silicon diodes, and other innovations included miniaturised electronic components, such as non-standard silicon chips tailored for individual customer needs. In 1956, Ferranti Ltd designed the Poseidon Computer, which was fitted into the aircraft carrier HMS *Eagle* as part of its Action Data Automation weapons' control system.

In 1958, the domestic appliances department, which had helped the company become a household name – not least with television sets rushed out so families could watch the 1953 coronation – was closed after becoming unprofitable. The decision was taken to concentrate on hi-tech products such as microwave communications and, after 1960, inertial navigation systems. The latter were used in Tornado aircraft and orbital satellites associated with the US Space Shuttle. In 1962 'the world's first process control computer' was installed by Ferranti Ltd at an ICI chemical plant, being itself a by-product of guided-missile technology.

Sebastian de Ferranti succeeded his father as chairman of Ferranti's in 1963, and continued the policy of innovation-led manufacture. He opened a micro-electronic assembly laboratory in Barrow-in-Furness, Lancashire, making integrated circuits and transistors for computers, electrical appliances and weapons' systems. The company also produced solar cells.

The mid-1970s were difficult times for British industry, with industrial relations at a low ebb. In 1974, Ferranti's required the financial aid

ABOVE Advertisments for early Ferranti domestic televisions.

of government, through the unlikely offices of Tony Benn, then Labour's industry minister. In return they gave the government a 50 per cent stake in Ferranti Ltd. This meant it was, in effect, part nationalised; Sebastian de Ferranti remained as chairman, but the family no longer had a controlling share.

In 1976, Ferranti Ltd supplied Total Oil Company with a new 'autocourt' fuel-dispensing system, which linked the self-operated pumps to the point-of-sale terminals – this system was later adopted by most garage operators.

RIGHT HM The Queen and HRH Prince Philip with Sebastian de Ferranti at the Ferranti's plant at South Gyle, near Edinburgh.

In 1980, the firm was fully returned to the private sector, with the government shareholding being placed with City institutions. In 1982, Sebastian de Ferranti stepped down as chairman after nineteen years, passing the chairmanship to his brother Basil, who had been M P for Morecambe and Lonsdale (1958–64), was currently M P for Hampshire West (1979–84), and subsequently M P for Hampshire Central from 1984 until his death in 1988. Basil de Ferranti also served as a Member of the European Parliament.

With global reach and employing more than twenty thousand people in Britain, in 1982 Ferranti's was floated on the stock market. In 1988 it was taken over by International Signals & Control, after which it entered stormy waters. In 1993 the company went into receivership. Sebastian de Ferranti said in 2000: 'It took a hundred years to establish our reputation and, in so many months, the then board destroyed it.'

LEFT A model of the Bloodhound missile, produced by Ferranti's for the British government from the late 1950s.

Londres '45

CHAPTER IV
SEBASTIAN DE FERRANTI: THE MAN & THE PATRON

IT TAKES A DREAMER TO CONCEIVE OF BUILDING SOMETHING out of the ordinary, and a dreamer with a strong grasp of the practical to see it through. Henbury Hall was the dream and delight of its imaginative and focused patron, Sebastian de Ferranti. He began this project in his fifties, after he had stepped down as the chairman of the family electronics and manufacturing company, an all-absorbing position to which he had dedicated all his skills and creativity. Thus the house became a new cause and conduit for his energies.

The project began to take serious shape after the death of his father, Sir Vincent, in 1980, and as Sebastian de Ferranti embarked on a new era, there is a sense that the house became part of the process of carving out a new identity. But he had explored other sketch ideas for the site, and indeed, had already, in 1977–78, remodelled a small farmhouse on the estate known as 'The Cave'. With advice from Felix Kelly, this had evolved into a romantic part-Palladian, part-Gothic 'eye-catcher'.

The new Henbury Hall, with its classical porticoed and domed temple form, was shaped by his experiences and embodied his love of life. An exuberant demonstration of the enduring appeal of the classical – especially the work of Palladio – the house was shaped by Sebastian de Ferranti's own rigorous interest in how things were designed and made. It reflects his delight in working alongside those skilled at design and making, something which can be traced back to his career in manufacturing. There can also be no doubt that he succeeded in gathering around him a 'ministry of all the talents'.

Sebastian de Ferranti is widely remembered for his energy, enthusiasm and sense of humour. A captain of industry from a young age, he was an

OPPOSITE A portrait of Sebastian de Ferranti as a young man, drawn by Annigoni in 1955.

early champion of micro-electronics and computer technology. He was the first industrialist to deliver a Granada Guildhall Lecture in the 1966 series – alongside Sir Kenneth Clark on art. De Ferranti spoke on 'Technology and Power', defining power as 'the capacity to prosper'. Articulate, funny and challenging, his lecture revealed an almost emotional connection to industry and innovation, something that led him to berate the editors of the *Encyclopaedia Britannica* for their focus on princes and politicians, and their failure to celebrate inventors and engineers.

Naturally, he had been brought up with a prodigious sense of the importance of inventors and engineers, not just to industry but also to civilisation. Born in October 1927, Sebastian de Ferranti grew up at Rose Hill House in Alderley Edge, a property his parents owned until they acquired the Henbury Hall estate in 1957. His life was steeped in the world of science, business and manufacture, and he was deeply proud of this part of his family's role in industry.

Sebastian de Ferranti was well travelled and energetic; he read widely, loved poetry, liked good food, and also took an interest in beautifully tailored clothes – he was once voted the best-dressed businessman in the UK. His son Hugo recalls that he had collected contemporary art for the Ferranti offices, including works by Bridget Riley, L. S. Lowry and Helen Bradley, but as he grew older, his interests became focused on nineteenth- and early twentieth-century masters.

Educated at the Roman Catholic school at Ampleforth Abbey, in Yorkshire, Sebastian de Ferranti won a place at Trinity College, Cambridge, but utterly depressed by the grey of post-war Britain, the appalling food and the cold, left during his first term, 'never to return'. Instead, he went on to do National Service as a commissioned officer in a cavalry regiment, the

BELOW LEFT An antique tester bed, bought by the teenage Sebastian de Ferranti with his pocket money, showing his early interest in finely made things.

BELOW RIGHT A Dragoon Guard's helmet, from Sebastian de Ferranti's period as an officer in the 4th/7th Royal Dragoon Guards.

4th/7th Dragoon Guards, in which he served from 1946 to 1948. The regiment had converted in the Second World War to light tanks and armoured reconnaissance, and Sebastian de Ferranti spent two years with them in Palestine, under Colonel R. A. Moulton-Barrett, 'a cavalryman of the old school', who had joined up in 1925.

This was during the difficult final years of the British mandate, following the UN resolution that Palestine should be divided. The role of the 4th/7th Dragoon Guards was to try and keep the peace between Jewish settlers (then arriving in great numbers, and including Holocaust survivors) and Palestinian Arabs. The army was in a strange position, with the British preparing for a withdrawal, but Sebastian de Ferranti seems to have found a sense of satisfaction in his role. A ceremonial helmet still stands in a case in Henbury Hall, and one of his stories that has become part of family lore is a memory of riding on beautiful clear Palestinian mornings, with 'the scent of wild hyacinths all around you'.

Back in civvy street, in 1950 Sebastian de Ferranti prepared to join the family firm, with placements at Brown Boveri of Switzerland and Alsthom of France. He became part of the Ferranti Transformer department and spent an intense period of assimilation of the art of transformer manufacture, where he developed a special interest in small-distribution transformers and set up a new process of mass production.

Joining the board of Ferranti in 1954, he was regarded as able and energetic. In 1958 he became managing director and in 1963 he succeeded his father, Sir Vincent, as chairman. While not without challenges, these were exciting years for the company, with expanding work on the Argus computers. Sebastian de Ferranti was committed to innovation; as he told the *New Scientist*, 'our policy remains to invest everything we've got to work on the frontiers of knowledge, so that we can really make a contribution to mankind.'

In 1982, Sebastian de Ferranti passed the chairmanship to his brother Basil, but he remained a significant Ferranti's shareholder and tried to

oppose the 1988 takeover which led the company to go into receivership in 1993. This was a bitter blow from which he never wholly recovered.

He remained very aware of the Ferranti workforce and his family's responsibility to them. According to his 2015 *Daily Telegraph* obituary, 'Sebastian, like his father and grandfather before him, always showed the greatest concern for his employees and inspired affection and loyalty in the company at all levels.' Later, when he had stepped down as chairman, he used to say 'a company is only another word for people – nothing else – just people', and that it was 'the people' he worked with that he really missed. He was proud of the 'outstanding group of exceptional engineers' the company had attracted during his own time in office.

Sebastian de Ferranti was also involved at director level in a number of other companies, including GEC, British Airways Helicopters and the National Nuclear Corporation. And he was, in addition, a public-spirited member of significant boards in the arts sector. He was a trustee of the Tate Gallery and chairman of the Civic Trust for the Northwest. He became a governor of the Royal Northern College of Music, and was chairman of the Hallé Concerts Society, presiding over the £42 million fundraising effort for the Bridgewater Hall, which opened in 1996 as a new home for the Hallé. His sense of public duty was displayed during his year as High Sheriff of Cheshire, in 1988, shortly after the completion of Henbury Hall. He was also one of the deputy lieutenants of the county.

Perhaps just as significant in terms of the shape and character of the house he built, he had a lifelong interest in country sports from early youth. When asked by their parents which schools they would like to attend, Basil de Ferranti chose Eton, but Sebastian chose Ampleforth, on account of the beauty of the surrounding countryside – and the beagle pack.

He loved sporting weekends in particular, and these sharpened his view of the amenities of the country estate and the country house. The journalist Chapman Pincher recalled enjoyable grouse shoots with Sebastian, where his host shared freely his insights into the then-tender relationship of government and industry.

Sebastian de Ferranti was a member of the famous Tarporley Hunt and hunted with them regularly. A keen polo player, he was Life President of the Cheshire Polo Club and had a full-size polo ground laid out at Henbury Hall – a considerable enterprise – to which the new house also formed a splendid backdrop. When he felt too old for these pursuits he took up carriage driving.

His love of polo, and later carriage driving, was shared with HRH Prince Philip, the Duke of Edinburgh, whom he came to know well, and who was a regular visitor to Henbury. So too were other members of the royal family. With HRH Prince Charles, Sebastian de Ferranti shared a love of classical architecture, and it was Prince Charles who was invited to lay the foundation stone of Henbury Hall.

In his long life, Sebastian de Ferranti was married three times and had four children. His much-loved brother, Basil, died on 24 September 1988, but Sebastian remained close to his sisters, Valerie, Prudence and Yolanda, and had a wide circle of friends. He kept up a voluminous correspondence. A few letters were handwritten, his writing an elegant italic; most were typed and signed; all were courteously expressed. His pleasure in good

OPPOSITE A global concern: Sebastian de Ferranti at the South Morang substation near Melbourne in Australia.

company and 'the good things in life' is evident in the memory of family and friends, and undoubtedly reflected in the house he built. Henbury Hall is brilliantly balanced between intimacy and elegance, and this balance is palpable in letters describing the evolution of the house, gardens and pool house, being a reflection of the man who conceived it.

Beatrice Saemann, who knew him from the 1940s, writes in 2018: 'He was unconventional and a lot of fun to be with. He was a good, reliable friend with a good sense of humour and we laughed a lot together in the early times when he visited with us in Switzerland in the mountains. He enjoyed being with people and also liked keeping contact with them.'

John Hardy, a former curator at the Victoria and Albert Museum, who knew Sebastian de Ferranti from his own Cheshire childhood, recalls: 'Sebastian had a wonderful chuckling laugh, and you could hear it all over the house – even coming up the stairs at Henbury and echoing in the dome. He also had wonderful manners. He was interested in art and had been a trustee for the Tate, but resigned. I think he had rather a good eye for paintings. He hugely enjoyed staying for shooting parties or polo at places such as Houghton and at Kedleston, and loved the richness of those buildings.'

He also recalls, 'Sebastian was not I think especially interested in architecture until he started the project. But once he began, he was addicted. He worried very much about the details, every single thing, from the width of the glazing bars to the lily in the frieze. The site is so good, and the house he built so very well crafted. Felix Kelly was especially wonderful in imagining attractive alterations to houses … Felix was very important to the development of the idea for Henbury.'

Other fellow Cheshire estate owners and neighbours remember him fondly too. Ricky Roundell, of Dorfold Hall, a vice-chairman of Christie's, recalls Sebastian as a 'larger than life character. He was ebullient and liked being the centre of attention, and quite enjoyed shocking people too. He was a life enhancer. The Henbury project certainly provoked a big interest in architecture. He wrote us a long letter about our plans to build a house, full of sensible suggestions. I think Henbury was a great reflection of him as a person.' Randle Brooks of Peover Hall, who knew him through playing polo in the 1950s, and shooting, says, 'he was full of enthusiasm, an optimist by nature, he was a thinking person too and a thoughtful companion.'

A hunting friend, Sarah Henderson, remembers him as 'over-generous always, with presents and tipping the staff, but always so well turned out in the field, always on the loveliest horses. A great guest, bringing lovely presents and writing thank-you letters, he was always very good fun, and very, very loyal. I think, too, he was a very private person underneath.'

Philippa de Pass, a friend through polo playing, says, 'Sebastian was always very amusing – and always good company. We knew him through polo, and met at Cowdray. He used to visit us at New Grove in his helicopter, landing on the paddock below the house blowing all the leaves around the garden, much to the fury of the gardeners. He could be very funny, but Sebastian could also be rather rude about one's food; he was very particular about food. He loved his polo – polo is really addictive.' Mrs de Pass adds, 'Above all, Sebastian was a very generous person, and always brought a thoughtful present when he came to visit, something like a beautiful limited edition book. I think Sebastian always lightened up any scene.'

In speaking to Sebastian de Ferranti's family and friends, a strong sense emerges of a man with a great zest for enjoyment, for friendship and for entertainment. He was a man who liked to know about things and to understand them. His daughter Camilla recalls how he always liked to understand how buildings worked best. Above all, he savoured friendship, and all his friends remember him as an unswervingly loyal friend, generous, entertaining and courteous. But he was a complex person too, more

RIGHT A pair of group portraits by Andrew Festing of the elite Tarporley Hunt Club, of which Sebastian de Ferranti was a long-term member. De Ferranti is seated on the extreme left of the far side on the table in the lower painting.

ABOVE LEFT Portrait of Sebastian de Ferranti seated in the morning room of the new Henbury Hall, painted by John Ward in 1998.

ABOVE RIGHT Gilly and Sebastian de Ferranti in front of Henbury Hall.

RIGHT Sebastian de Ferranti, a keen country sportsman, riding to hounds.

private than many people thought, a voracious reader and a deep thinker. A Roman Catholic, he had a strong religious faith, and attended Mass most Sundays even when away from home. This gave him a strong moral compass and his faith meant more to him than perhaps people realised.

He had worked at the forefront of British technology through expansive but difficult times, and it was perhaps this harder edge that made his pleasure in the architectural project all the more keen. He liked to enjoy Henbury Hall to the full, take tea in his dressing room with its fine views, dine on the south portico in the shade on a hot day, or watch the sunset through the tall windows. His widow, Gilly de Ferranti, recalls, 'Henbury Hall gave him an enormous amount of pleasure; he loved it unreservedly. He liked to use every room, every day, whether entertaining or not. It's really a very easy house to live in and to enjoy.'

Those who worked with him remember his interest and recognised his restless but decisive nature. They all recall how he savoured the building process and the decorating that followed. His architect, Julian Bicknell, remembers especially the parties he gave for all the builders and their families: 'The clients who fall in love with architecture tend to be the ones who know the names of everyone involved.' Dick Reid, the York carver who worked on Henbury Hall in the 1980s, summed up the presence of the patron: 'He was an enthusiast.' Pure and simple.

ABOVE Gilly and Sebastian de Ferranti following a meet of hounds at Henbury from the estate buggy in 2014.

CHAPTER V
THE PATH TO HENBURY: PALLADIO & THE PALLADIANS

HENBURY HALL IS BOTH A WORK OF ART AND A HOUSE TO LIVE in. Its design was intended to follow the vision of the classical as unfolded in the work of Andrea Palladio (1508–1580): a reflection of ancient Rome reinterpreted and reinvented for its own time. As David Watkin says in his 1986 *History of Western Architecture*, Palladio's work 'has been valued for centuries as the quintessence of High Renaissance calm and harmony.'

The fame of Palladio derived from his interpretation of classical architecture for a thoroughly businesslike class of merchant princes, based in Vicenza and Venice; and his career was much helped along by influential and intellectual friends. 'Palladianism' – like so many art historical terms – is much debated. It is used to embrace a wide range of seventeenth- and early eighteenth-century design. But they are all inspired, in essence, by the pursuit of the same classical ideal.

Palladianism introduces us to the broad notion of harmonious, austere classical elevations that rely more on proportion than decoration for effect and that look back to the classical tradition of the later Renaissance as exemplified by the work of Palladio. Palladio's buildings and his publications were, without doubt, pre-eminent among the preferred reference points of the mid-eighteenth-century, connoisseur-minded patron class who shaped the vision of the English country house.

Palladio, who trained as a practical stonemason, enjoyed huge success in his own time. He built a large number of villas, palaces, churches and theatres, 'after the antique' (*all' antica*). To the merchant princes and their clerical and civic counterparts, he gave buildings which demonstrated the fundamentals of antique architecture, propriety, order and proportion, and which also 'worked' for their needs. These principles of ancient

OPPOSITE Portrait of Andrea Palladio by an unknown sixteenth-century artist.

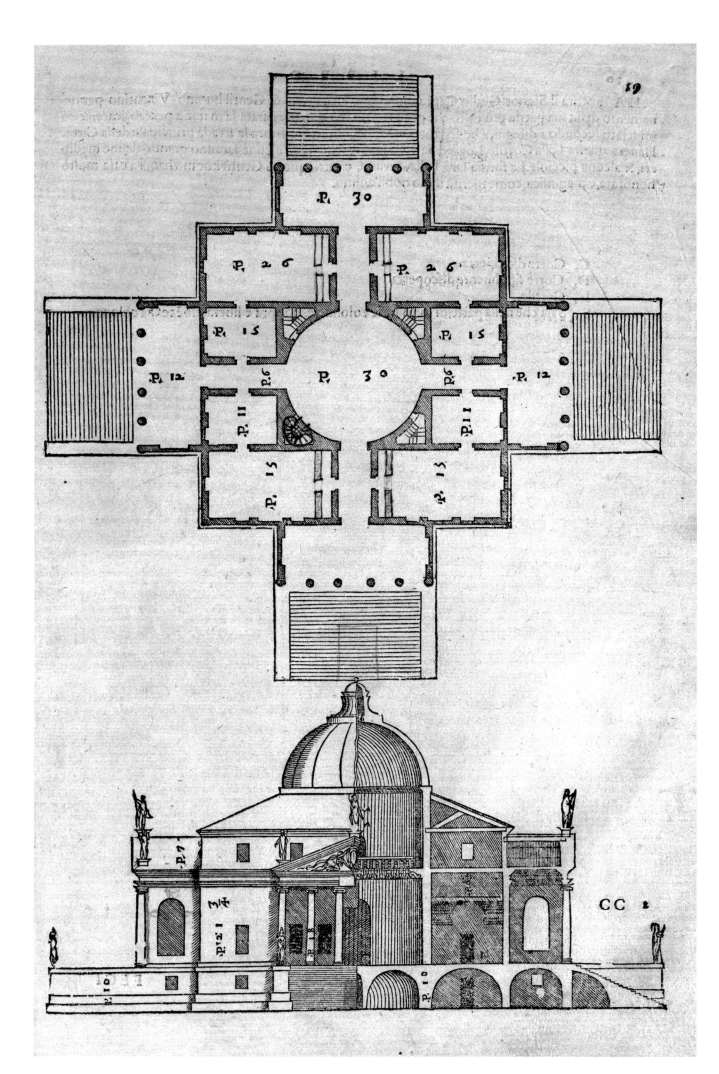

architecture he had studied in the treatise of Marcus Vitruvius Pollo, the first-century BC Roman architect-engineer, and also in the ruined survivals of the great Roman age to which he devoted much attention and 'very great fatigues and voyages'. Palladio was one of the first to measure ancient ruins and work out the principles of their design.

Even more important than his extensive output were the engravings created for his four volumes *I quattro libri dell'architettura*. These illustrated reconstructed antique architecture alongside his own designs in the classical spirit. Published (from 1570) and republished, translated and circulated, the books' illustrations provided a compelling and engaging source of plans, elevations and ornament.

It is in large part through these books that Palladio's ideas became such a dominant force. As architectural historian James Ackerman wrote in 1966: 'All over the western world, hundreds of thousands of houses, churches and public buildings with symmetrical fronts and applied half columns topped by a pediment descend from the designs of Palladio. He is the most imitated architect in history.'

Through his written work, Palladio became the model for Inigo Jones, court architect (as well as designer of masques) to the Stuarts in England. Jones designed the Banqueting House in Whitehall and advised on Wilton House in Wiltshire. Travelling through Italy, he annotated by hand his own copies of *I quattro libri* – while also eagerly acquiring original Palladio drawings.

OPPOSITE Plan and section of Palladio's most famous villa, known as La Rotonda or the Villa Capra, as illustrated in his *I quattro libri*; it was begun in 1566, and completed some thirty years later.

BELOW La Rotonda seen from above; the dome as built was different from the dome as published.

ABOVE La Rotonda enjoys an attractive and pleasing rural setting, just on the edge of Vicenza.

The gentleman amateur Sir Roger Pratt, writing in the 1660s, advised those desirous of building a house to consult some 'ingenious gentleman who has seen much of that kind abroad and been somewhat versed in the best authors of Architecture: viz. Palladio, Scamozzi etc'. Alongside Palladio's *I quattro libri*, Pratt also appears to cite *L'idea dell'architettura universale* (1615) by Vincenzo Scammozzi, an architect who completed several of Palladio's projects after his death (and whom Inigo Jones met on his travels in Italy).

I quattro libri was used by the post-Restoration generation of Wren, Hawksmoor and Vanbrugh. A 1650 French edition is one of the few books we actually know that Vanbrugh owned, and there is a copy in the Castle Howard library with annotations thought to be in Vanbrugh's hand.

Most importantly, the books became a valued touchstone of architectural discipline and reference for the neo-Palladians, such as the 3rd Earl of Burlington (1694–1753), his collaborator William Kent, and the architect Colen Campbell, who championed 'Antique Simplicity' in architecture.

Burlington acquired a number of Palladio's actual surveys of the baths of ancient Rome and had them published in 1730, as *Fabbriche antiche disegnate da Andre Palladio vicentino*, which had a demonstrable effect on the design and planning of the English country house and public buildings alike. William Kent, who worked at Holkham Hall in Norfolk in the 1720s and 1730s, produced what is considered the fullest expression of the influence of the Palladian model on English taste. Holkham Hall is, as David Watkin wrote, 'a pure work of art, conceived as a shrine for paintings and sculpture specifically bought for it in Italy by Lord Leicester'.

The Palladian idiom, in part represented by the plans and elevations illustrated in *I quattro libri*, came to define the very image of the English country house in the eighteenth century. It went on to play a significant role in American architecture, too. In 1816, Colonel Isaac A. Coles recorded a conversation with the President, Thomas Jefferson, during which they 'conversed at length on the subject of architecture'. Palladio, Jefferson said, 'was the Bible – you should get it and stick close to it.'

Palladio's story deserves attention if we are to understand the story of Henbury Hall, with its references to both the sixteenth-century Italian vision of the ideal classical villa and to the eighteenth-century interpretations of that model in England. Palladio's vision of the life of the villa, revealed in phrases shaped by his awareness of classical literature, has an appeal all of its own. To him, villas were places where men 'fatigued by the agitations of the city, will be greatly restored and comforted, and be able quietly to attend to the studies of letters and contemplation.'

Born in 1508, Palladio was, as Ackerman reminds us, 'a contemporary and collaborator of Veronese, Tintoretto and the sculptor Vittoria, and died only three years after Titian.' These names all bring to mind rich colour, light and texture – 'peculiarly Venetian luxuries for which Palladio came to invent the architectural equivalents'.

Christened Andrea di Pietro della Gondola, Palladio was apprenticed to a sculptor in Padua at the age of thirteen. In 1524, he moved to Padua, where he spent fourteen years as apprentice and assistant to Giovanni de Pedemuro and Girolamo Pittoni, who dominated work on Verona's sculpture and monuments. Working as a mason on the Villa Trissino at Cricoli, outside Vicenza, in the 1530s, he came to the attention of humanist scholar Count Gian Giorgio Trissino. Trissino gave him the classical-sounding new name of 'Palladio' and introduced him to classical literature, including the works of Vitruvius.

Trissino gathered young aristocrats about him in an academy devoted to the study of classical literature, philosophy and mathematics. Many of these aristocrats went on to become Palladio's clients. The young Palladio had more than talent; he had charm. His earliest biography, Paolo Gualdo's *Vita di Andrea Palladio* (1616), made special note of this: 'He developed a very close relationship with the Vicentine humanist Gian Giorgio Trissino, one of the greatest scholars of his time. Finding Palladio to be a young man of very spirited character and with a great aptitude for science and mathematics, Trissino encouraged his natural abilities by training him in the precepts of Vitruvius.'

In around 1540, Palladio designed the Villa Godi, at Lonedo, and a palazzo in Vicenza for the Civena family. He visited Rome in 1541 and 1547 to study ancient ruins and the works of Renaissance masters, including the Tempietto by Bramante and Raphael's Villa Madama. He later recalled that he found the ruins of Rome 'much more worthy of observation than I first realised'. In 1554–56 he was again in Rome, and published a guide to its monuments, *L'Antichità di Roma*, which became a standard reference work. In 1556, he assisted the classical scholar Daniele Barbaro with his illustrations for an edition of Vitruvius.

The influence on his work of his visits to Rome is seen in a greater simplicity in his design approach and the reduction of reference to the work of other contemporary architects. His well-judged manipulation of interior volume, and keen sense of the effect of integrated architecture, might

also be traced to his first-hand study of Roman bath complexes. His first great public commission was to reconstruct the exterior of the Basilica at Vicenza, in 1546–49. The nobility of Vicenza proved to be some of his most significant early patrons: the Palazzo Thiene at Santo Stefano followed in 1546, and the Palazzo Valmarana – with giant order pilasters echoing Michelangelo's Capitoline palaces – in 1565–66.

The Venetian nobility of the sixteenth century were actively buying up and draining the land of the Veneto for more productive agriculture, much of it based on millet, a new grain crop that had been introduced from the Americas. Palladio famously designed numerous villa farms for them, including the Villa Barbaro at Maser (around 1560) with its central temple front and wings of barns linked by arcades in the Roman antique manner.

Based on the model of surviving Roman examples from temples, the portico became one of the most familiar themes in Palladio's work. In the sixteenth century, it was assumed that some examples had come from villas and palaces, and the crisp giant order portico became the defining feature of the villas of the 1550s and 1560s. These include the Villa Pisani at Montagna and the Villas Badoer, Chiercati, Emo, Foscari and Cornaro. In all of these examples, Palladio presented variations on a theme of the pedimented portico and two-storey villa with colonnades, or symmetrically arranged loggias. (One of his last and most celebrated buildings, La Rotonda, will be considered in detail later – see opposite, and following pages.)

Palladio is also known for his magnificent churches in Venice. He designed the main facades for San Francesco della Vigna (1568–92), San Giorgio Maggiore (begun 1565) and Il Redentore (1577–92). These domed edifices feature facades with interlocking pedimented temple fronts and engaged columns, inspired by Palladio's own reconstruction of the Basilica di Massenzio (Maxentius). They are designed on unusual plans which reflect the need to accommodate additional choirs for special events, with a monastic choir located behind a screen of columns.

San Giorgio Maggiore was an important place for Sebastian de Ferranti, as the church contains the tombs of his Ziani ancestors. Another idealised Pantheon-form church is found in the Tempietto at Maser, for Marc Antonio Barbaro, and one of Palladio's greatest, and last, works was the Teatro Olimpico in Vicenza, completed by Scamozzi in the 1580s.

Palladio's villas belonged to a particular moment in the story of Vicenza and the Venetian republic. His working life coincided with a period of peace and inward investment in reclamation and landed estates. The accompanying proliferation of country houses and villa farms has been referred to by some historians as a kind of 're-feudalization'.

Houses of this region traditionally had a central atrium or open loggia and, from the mid-sixteenth century, began to be designed and decorated self-consciously in the spirit of classical villas, as shown by works by Sanmicheli and Sansovino. Palladio's inspired villa designs were a continuation of this search for classical expression; many are variations of different tripartite compositions with a central block on the axis of its entrance and symmetrical pavilion wings.

The search for order and balance reflected ideas about beauty. A contemporary mathematician, Silvio Belli, wrote in 1573 that beauty was defined by 'a correspondence of all parts arranged in their proper place'. Extending to three dimensions, the proportional systems used by Palladio to calculate the relationship of parts were echoed in musical (and mathematical) theory. Aiming at harmonic proportions, Palladio saw a parallel between musical and spatial ratios – which derived from a reading of classical theorists.

The units in Palladio's drawings are generally Vicentine feet (*piedi vicentini*) but the actual length of a foot varied from place to place. Scammozzi's *post facto* measured drawings make it clear that the buildings as executed are rarely entirely accurate, but the proportional principles are maintained – principally as an aid to the builders. Palladio, as a practical builder, knew that a simple proportional base made things more straightforward for the builders on site.

Palladio continued to be well liked by his contemporaries. His biographer Paolo Gualdo wrote: 'Palladio was very agreeable and witty in conversation, much to the relish of the gentlemen and signori with whom he dealt, but also to workers whose services he enlisted. Always keeping their spirits up by entertaining them with many pleasantries, he made them work in good cheer.'

LA ROTONDA

More than four centuries later, Henbury Hall was consciously designed as a homage to Palladio's work. Julian Bicknell recalls: 'The technology of design we used was no more sophisticated than Palladio's – pen and pencil on paper backed up by arithmetic and geometry.'

Palladio's influence has been explored, but the significance of La Rotonda – or Villa Capra – requires a more detailed consideration. Of all his villas, La Rotonda has been viewed as the finest demonstrations of an 'ideal' classical villa, a direct evocation of the house as conceived of by the ancients. Of course, we now also see it as an evocation mediated through the sixteenth-century humanist vision of the Roman past.

Built for a scholarly priest, Cardinal Paolo Almerico, starting in 1567, La Rotonda stands on an eminence about a mile and a half from the centre of Vicenza. With each face a pedimented portico, hexastyle – that is to say, with six columns – the villa has a low tiled dome as its crown. It is a symmetrical building, its geometric form a perfect circle inside a square.

OPPOSITE A section and elevation of La Rotonda, with its hexastyle (six column) portico fronts, from *Andrea Palladio's architecture in four books* (London, 1736).

'Cool, stately, without a trace of pomposity, its four lovely porticoes look down to the north, south, east and west on to the olive groves and vineyards of the Veneto, all ripening in the sun,' was how John Julius Norwich memorably captured the spirit of La Rotonda in *Spirit of the Age* (1975). The sense of connection to the land in this building was – and is – palpable. Even from the inner central domed hall, the pastoral landscape can be seen.

In the words of a 1736 translation of *I quattro libri* (*Andrea Palladio's architecture in four books*), 'The site is as pleasant and delightful as can be found, because it is upon a small hill, of very easy access, and is watered on one side by the Bacchiglione, a navigable river, and on the other side is encompassed by most pleasant risings which look like a very great theatre, and are well cultivated, and abound with most excellent fruits and most exquisite vines.'

Palladio's words make clear the significance of the setting – the eminence, the wider views, the fertile landscape and the water were all vital to the impact of his idealised villa. He adds: 'Therefore as it enjoys from every part most beautiful views, some of which are limited, some more extended, others that terminate with the horizon, there are loggias made in all four of the fronts.'

The spaces under the porticoes (and the basement level) were 'the rooms of convenience' for household and everyday use, while on the main *piano nobile*, 'the hall is in the middle, is round, and receives its light from above' (as Palladio himself recounts). The interior was richly decorated with stucco work, by the same *stuccatori* who worked on the Teatro Olimpico (the painted decoration is seventeenth century).

La Rotonda was not built alongside farm buildings but as a *villa suburbana*, a place of retreat and entertainment (half town house, half country house). Paolo Almerico was a scholar-priest of wealth and influence from an aristocratic family. As a younger son, he looked for a career in the Church and was appointed – at the age of fourteen – as a canon of the cathedral in Vicenza. While studying in Padua, he paid for a new portal for the cathedral, designed by Palladio. In 1560–66 he was in Rome as a papal court official, after which he acquired an estate near Vicenza. Although habitable by June 1569, La Rotonda was not entirely complete when Almerico died in 1589.

La Rotonda was hugely admired from the start; educated visitors immediately recognised the link to the Pantheon in Rome. The domed central hall is the central planning element from which the wider plan evolves. The dome as finished – low, tiled and Roman in character – is different from that published by Palladio in *I quattro libri* in 1570. Which version did Palladio intend? We cannot know; but it may well have been completed

XV

E. Hoppus delin.

B. Cole sculp

in this manner for practical reasons, as it must surely be the case that the published version represented Palladio's vision of the ideal classical villa.

This form continued the search for a perfect building that gripped earlier Renaissance artists and designers. It was inspired in part by the Pantheon in Rome, which Palladio had studied closely, and had been prefigured by the Casa Mantegna, Mantua (1476–1502), built for and possibly to designs by the painter Andrea Mantegna. Palladio was also influenced by the works of Brunelleschi, Alberti and Bramante, who all endeavoured to identify perfect geometrical proportions.

Palladio explored the form further in designs for a villa for the Trissino family at Meledo, with a rotunda between colonnades and pavilion outbuildings (sadly only partly realised). It should be noted that the dome at La Rotonda was designed to be open, in the manner of the Pantheon's dome (but was later glazed in).

The admiration for La Rotonda persists. As Bruce Boucher observed in 1998, 'Posterity has paid the architect the compliment of elevating the Rotonda into the realm of a cult object like the Pantheon or the *Mona Lisa*, a confirmation one could say, of its status as a classic. Above all, the Rotonda embodied a lifelong pursuit of an ideal, a vision of antiquity not so much rediscovered in the ruins of Rome as re-created in Palladio's mind.'

THE PALLADIANS

The influence of Palladio on English designers was profound and potent, although the domed rotunda form did not feature in the interpretations of Inigo Jones, despite his having visited La Rotonda. However, the domed villa form, and symmetrical plan, became of additional interest to the later generations of the seventeenth and eighteenth centuries.

By no means an architect considered a 'Palladian' by architectural historians, Sir John Vanbrugh produced probably the most remarkable homage to La Rotonda in the park at Castle Howard. Although by experience a leading figure of the English baroque, he was conscious of the increasing interest in Palladio's *I quattro libri* among the younger generation, educated by the Grand Tour.

Vanbrugh famously created a park temple at Castle Howard in Yorkshire as a belvedere, a place of retreat to enjoy company and the views, which later became known as the Temple of the Four Winds. Built in 1727–28, it is a diminutive, scaled-down version of La Rotonda, and was part of the landscaping project for Lord Carlisle. Hawksmoor, Vanbrugh's assistant on the project, wrote, in January 1724, 'I know Sir J. Vanbrugh is for a Temple of smooth freestone with a portico each way, and Dom'd over the Center.'

At Lord Carlisle's request, Hawksmoor provided an alternative; but Vanbrugh remained steadfast and, in February 1724, he wrote to Lord Carlisle, 'The first Design I sent, with the 4 porticoes will be found very near (perhaps quite) as cheap, as any Gothick Tower … My Lord Morpeth [Carlisle's eldest son] about a Month ago, View'd all the Designs I had sent, He declar'd his thoughts utterly against anything but an Italian Building in

BELOW Sir John Vanbrugh's 1720s belvedere, later known as the Temple of the Four Winds, at Castle Howard was an undoubted homage to 'Italian' style in the form of a miniaturised version of La Rotonda.

that Place, and entirely approv'd the Design [by which he meant one in the spirit of Palladio].'

Much reduced in scale from Palladio's model, with tetrastyle (four-column) porticoes, and no first floor, Castle Howard's park temple is widely considered one of the purest homages to Palladio's masterpiece, illustrating Vanbrugh's evolution as an architect, as well his eye on the rising tide of Grand Tour taste in the younger generation of connoisseur-minded patrons. It was a taste focused more and more on the harmonious proportions of Palladio's interpretations, and the exemplars which he so usefully gave in his published – executed and unexecuted – designs.

The year 1715 was important for the 'Palladian' story in Britain. In this year Colen Campbell published the first volume of his three-volume *Vitruvius Britannicus*, a work on contemporary classically inspired architecture that placed the model of Palladio centre stage. Indeed, he was specifically held up as one 'who has exceeded all that were gone before him, and surpassed his contemporaries; whose ingenious labours will eclipse many, and rival most, of the Ancients.' In the same year, Giacomo Leoni brought out *The Four Books of Architecture*, a version of *I quattro libri* in English (with 'necessary corrections with respect to Shading, Dimensions, Ornaments, etc.', which meant it was not considered the best source by Burlington's circle). Isaac Ware's *The Four Books on Architecture* in 1738 was a more faithful English translation of Palladio's original.

Lord Burlington designed himself a rotunda, or a domed and porticoed villa, alongside his existing Jacobean house at Chiswick. It was, in effect, a pleasure pavilion for the display of art – or, as Lord Norwich put it in 1975: 'a pavilion of the spirit, in which to surround himself with beauty – books and paintings and sculpture, all in a setting of immaculate Palladian proportions'.

It was in some ways a variant on La Rotonda's form, with only one portico face, but while long thought of as principally a homage to Palladio, it draws much of its reference from Scammozzi's Villa Rocca Pisana, with its

BELOW LEFT Portrait of Lord Burlington by Jonathan Richardson; in the background is the 'Bagnio' he designed for his gardens at Chiswick House.

BELOW RIGHT Chiswick House, designed by Lord Burlington, and drawing on Palladio's La Rotonda and Scammozzi's Villa Rocca Pisana.

low dome and recessed portico (*in antis*). Horace Walpole was critical of Chiswick's 'too strict adherence to the rules of symmetry', a Palladian trait, but also thought it was overall 'a model of taste ... more worth seeing than many fragments of ancient grandeur, which our travellers visit under all the dangers attendant on long voyages'.

William Kent (1685–1748), who trained as a painter in Italy for ten years, from 1709 to 1719, assisted in the development of Burlington's design when he returned to England. He was responsible for the rich decoration of the interiors of Chiswick, which reflect his years of training in Rome.

The Scottish architect Colen Campbell (1676–1729) designed one of the most faithful of the English neo-Palladian homages to La Rotonda, the 27-metre (88-feet) square Mereworth Castle in Kent. It was built for Colonel Fane (later 7th Earl of Westmorland) in 1723–25, around a dramatic central circular hall with dome and lantern, with a hexastyle portico to each face. Campbell himself pointed out how warm the house was: 'there are but Four Chimneys, which are brought up by Four obelisks ... there is a strong brick Arch that brings 24 Funnels to a Lanthorn, which

ABOVE An aerial view of Mereworth Castle, an exacting reproduction of La Rotonda built in 1723–25 for Colonel Fane. The two wings were added twenty years later.

BELOW AND
OPPOSITE Section and
elevation of Mereworth
Castle, Kent, as published
in *Vitruvius Britannicus*
vol. III, 1725.

is finished with a copper Callot ... not the least difficult part of the design.'

John Loveday, a visitor in 1730, commented: 'Colonel Fane, Brother
to the Earl of Westmorland, has built an Italian House at Merryworth,
with great expence. You ascend to it by a great flight of Stone Steps, under
which are part of the Offices. A vast Portico on every side of the House,
so that there are four Fronts exactly alike, but Steps up to only one. The
Windows are very small. A Cupolo very large, seemingly too large for the
size of the House, as are also the Porticoes. The Rooms below are lofty,
above very low.' He also noted the slick hiding of the chimneys.

Designed by Thomas Wright, Nuthall Temple in Nottinghamshire was
built in 1754 for Sir Charles Sedley. This rotunda was perhaps even more
closely modelled on Scammozzi's Villa Rocca Pisana, with pedimented
hexastyle recessed portico to the east and a domed roof. The central hall
was octagonal and adorned with rich plasterwork. When its last occupant,
the Reverend Robert Holden, died in 1926, his son made several attempts
to sell it. He succeeded in 1929, but its contents were stripped, then the
empty shell sold for £800 to J. H. Brough of Beeston. He presided over
a public demolition at which 'the west wing was loaded with firelighters,
sprinkled with paraffin and set alight to the delight of the expectant crowd.'

Also in 1754, Foot's Cray Place in Kent was built for one Bourchier
Cleeve, with a hexastyle Ionic portico to each elevation, and the whole
crowned by a hemispherical dome with tall tapering chimneys. This was
once attributed to Isaac Ware, but is now thought to have been designed

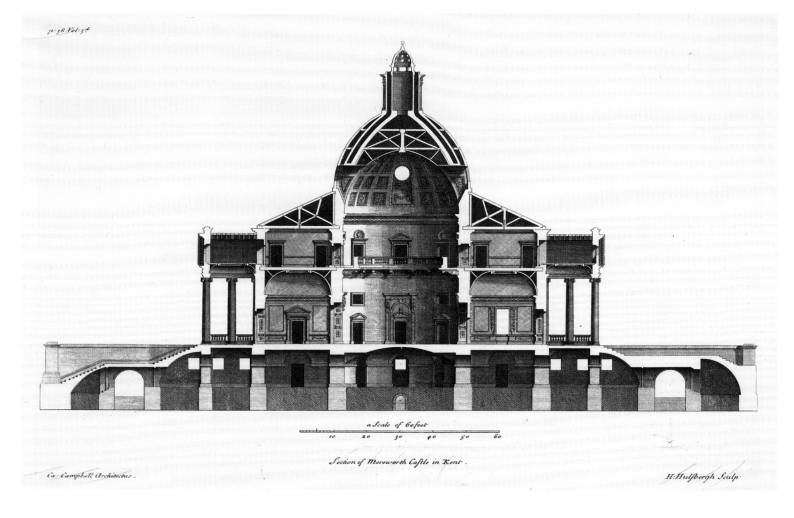

Section of Mereworth Castle in Kent.

Ca: Campbell Architectus.

a Scale of 60 feet

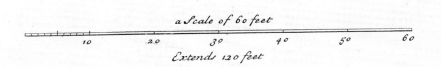

10   20   30   40   50   60

Extends 120 feet

The Elevation of Merenvorth Castle near Maidstone in Kent
the Seat of the Honourable Iohn Fane Esqr:

H. Hulfbergh Sculp:

by Daniel Garrett (Ware may have completed it after Garrett's death). A contemporary noted of Foot's Cray Place that it was 'built after a design of Palladio of the Ionic order, and is peculiarly elegant. The original design had four porticoes, three of which are filled up to gain more room. The hall is octagonal, and has a gallery, ornamented with busts leading to the bed-chambers. It is enlightened from the top and is very beautiful.' Damaged by fire in 1949, it was demolished shortly afterwards.

The rotunda form, the domed villa, represented an ideal of a sort, but few attempts were made in England to reproduce it during the Palladian heyday, and only Mereworth and Chiswick survive, along with Vanbrugh's individualistic Palladian essay at Castle Howard. The pantheonic form was an important influence on the development of neoclassical taste, and was expressed in later buildings such as Belle Isle in the Lake District and Ickworth Park in Suffolk – as well as Thomas Jefferson's Monticello and Virginia State Capitol in the United States. These buildings bear a family resemblance. They were not dependent on Palladian sources alone, instead drawing widely on antique and Renaissance models. But they all suggest the enduring appeal of the classical forms, and the combined elegance of dome and portico.

Henbury Hall was inspired by Palladio, and to some extent by Vanbrugh's Temple of the Four Winds, and the artist Felix Kelly's wonderful insight into those buildings. While undoubtedly drawing inspiration from La Rotonda, it departs from it in several critical ways: the porticoes step out much further from the central cube, and are conspicuously enriched in contrast to the plain cube; the windows effectively fill the wall within the porticoes.

Henbury Hall was also inspired by a more diffuse sense of the connection between the classically inspired porticoed mansion and the verdant, rolling landscaped park associated with the world of the Georgian country house. It is a vision that projects an idea of the civilised way of life across the centuries, the embodiment of harmony and calm – qualities which appealed deeply and profoundly to a worldly wise British industrialist, deeply interested in the 'Palladian' story, and just as proud of his own Venetian heritage.

ABOVE LEFT Nuthall Temple, Nottinghamshire, demolished in 1929.

ABOVE RIGHT Foot's Cray Place, Kent, built in 1754, possibly to designs of Daniel Garrett (closely following Mereworth Castle, except with filled-in porticoes).

FOLLOWING PAGES Henbury Hall, seen from the north, draws on the inspiration of both the original Palladio-designed models and the Anglo-Palladian eighteenth-century versions.

LEFT The interior of Nuthall Temple, designed by Thomas Wright in 1754.

CHAPTER VI
THE DESIGNERS

SEBASTIAN DE FERRANTI SOUGHT OUT THE ADVICE AND SERVICES of several talented designers, each of whom contributed to the evolution of the design. Most published accounts of Henbury Hall tend to overlook the earliest phases.

MINORU YAMASAKI

There is little in the family papers to help elucidate the often-repeated story of Sebastian de Ferranti's early approach to Minoru Yamasaki (1912–1986), the Japanese-American architect whose career had begun in the office of the firm of Shreve, Lamb & Harmon, who had designed the Empire State Building. Yamasaki is best known for his Twin Towers (the World Trade Centre) in New York City, and regarded by historians as a 'New Formalist' (certainly with no interest in Brutalism). But Sebastian de Ferranti himself noted that the appeal for him was more in Yamasaki's original response to historic architecture in his own undeniably Modernist vision (and he appears to have been thinking in particular of buildings such as the Federal Science Pavilion at the World's Fair in Seattle in 1962).

Dale Allen Guyre in *Minoru Yamasaki: Humanist Architecture for a Modernist World* (2017) records that Yamasaki 'secured a place in post-war architectural history through designs that captured the exuberant optimism of late fifties– early sixties America by merging technological proficiency and smooth elegance with exotic (and hybrid) influences from distant lands.' These earlier buildings were popular, 'enticing, photogenic, and very different from the mainstream'.

But, sadly, no drawings, designs or correspondence survive at Henbury Hall to explain how this design actually might have looked, although we

OPPOSITE A delicious imaginary *capriccio* painting by Felix Kelly of a domed classical rotunda with a tetrastyle (four-columned) Ionic portico, typical of his neo-Romantic imaginings.

RIGHT Minoru Yamasaki, the Japanese-American architect Sebastian de Ferranti approached for more Modernist-inspired designs for the new Henbury Hall.

have Sebastian de Ferranti's recorded view that such a scheme did not seem right in this particular landscape setting. It might be assumed that this dialogue took place in the late 1960s.

JOHN TAYLOR

The earliest sketches that actually survive for a new building at Henbury Hall on the site of the old house were done in the mid-1970s, by an architect friend and neighbour in London, John Taylor (1928–1998). Taylor, a founder partner of Chapman Taylor Partners, was educated at Stowe and studied architecture at Cambridge and the Architectural Association. He worked for Guy Morgan in the mid-1950s and it was in that office that he met Bob Chapman and Jane Durham. In 1959 they left to set up their own practice, Chapman Taylor Partners, which was highly successful and well respected. Taylor had a great love of old buildings and landscape, and led the firm into masterplanning for the Grosvenor, Crown and Cadogan Estates and the Church Commissioners.

His heroes were architects such as John Campbell, Clough Williams-Ellis and Edwin Lutyens, in whose work 'he admired a unique response to context and a bold use of natural materials exploiting light and shade, coupled with an undoubted degree of eccentricity'. Taylor's wide-ranging output included Caxton House, Tothill Street, Westminster, for Commercial Union Properties (1979) and Lansdowne House, Berkeley Square, for Legal & General Assurance (1985). His own house was a stone-built castle in Wales, designed in an eighteenth-century spirit.

Sebastian de Ferranti clearly had asked Taylor for ideas, and Taylor came up with what he called, in a letter of 6 December 1976, 'a utility Palladian villa to be built on the site of the old house'. It was a 'a very simple square plan round a reasonably large central hall lit by a glass dome'. He suggested: 'You [might] alter your lifestyle and eat in the kitchen. It would be possible to dine in the hall, and it would also make a magnificent picture gallery. Only four doors lead off this hall, all centrally placed, giving access to the two bedroom "suites" and the drawing room. The drawing room is large and somewhere within it or adjacent to it there would be a staircase down to the cellars and the vaulted study.'

The intended orientation was for the main drawing room and master bedroom to face the park (south-west and south-east respectively). The boiler room and other functions were to be located in the existing old cellar. He thought it could all be done for £75,000, and perhaps a simple version for £50,000 – which was reiterated in a letter from the quantity surveyors, Gardiner & Theobald, of 9 December 1976, where the outline costings were explained more carefully (and with allowances for finishing but nothing 'lavish'). The sketch showed a plan 15 metres (50 feet) square surrounded by an arcade, with the central square hall (6 × 6 metres/20 × 20 feet) lit only from a clerestory in a central dome.

On 18 December, he wrote again, reviewing, with a long list of pros and cons, the options for a new house for the estate, including the extension of The Cave, which he thought was 'the least expensive alternative', but would always be too small for 'gracious entertaining' – which reveals Sebastian de Ferranti's priorities for a new house (also given the context of Sir Vincent

BELOW Letter and sketch from architect John Taylor in 1976, envisaging a 'utility Palladian villa', a new single-storey pavilion house on the site.

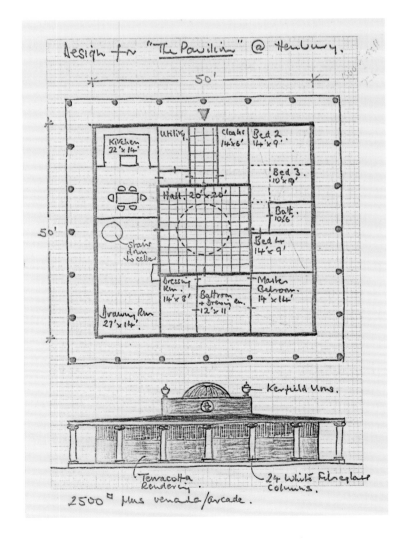

and Lady de Ferranti still being resident in the Tenants' Hall). Taylor also thought the Tenants' Hall 'wrongly sited' and 'awkwardly planned'.

For a new pavilion on the site of the old house along the lines of his sketched proposal, Taylor wrote out a long list of points which included:

FOR   a. You get all the accommodation you need.
       b. Gracious living possible.
       c. Cheapest to run and maintain.
       d. You need a 'folly' on the estate.
       e. The site is superb.
       f. You can achieve the perfect compact plan.
       g. No gardening, just a few Versailles tubs.
       h. No garages or stabling needed as they are readily accessible.
       i. You will improve the Estate.

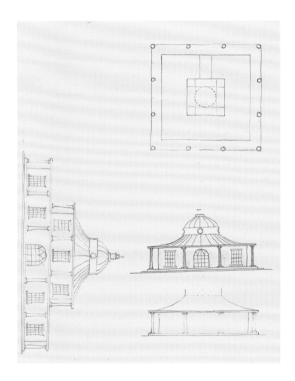

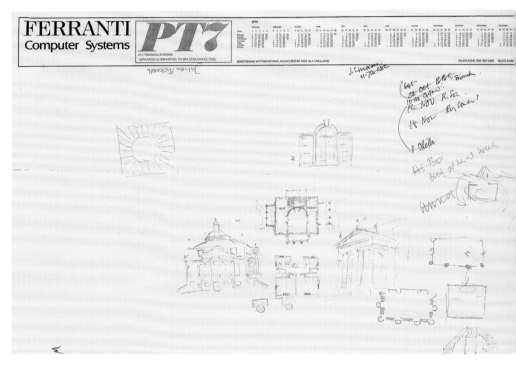

ABOVE Thinking out loud: early sketches of the design for Henbury Hall on Ferranti computer desk pads.

A letter of 15 December 1976 suggested exploring the conversion of the cellars alone, with a new dome on top. At this point, Taylor seemed to step back and a new artist collaborator took the stage.

FELIX KELLY

Perhaps the most crucial figure in the narrative of Henbury's conception and design was the artist and set designer Felix Kelly (1914–1994). Best known for his distinctive paintings of houses in the 1980s and 1990s, in this period he also advised on architecture. As well as his work on Henbury Hall in the early 1980s, his sketches became the basis for the renovation of Prince Charles's house Highgrove, in Gloucestershire, in 1986–87.

Kelly was born in Auckland, New Zealand, the son of a surveyor and a painter, and moved to London in his twenties. He worked as a graphic artist in advertising (including for Lintas, part of Unilever) until 1939, when he joined the RAF. However, this did not stem the flow of his art;

RIGHT Views of London by Felix Kelly in the collection at Henbury.

during the war he exhibited alongside Lucian Freud, Graham Sutherland, John Piper and Frances Hodgkins, and was counted as part of the New Romantic movement.

His first solo show was at London's Lefevre Gallery in 1943. His paintings – influenced in part by the Surrealist movement – were admired by Herbert Read, a champion of Modern Movement painting and author of an enthusiastic introduction to a 1946 book on Kelly's work. Read said that Kelly 'has obviously been influenced by our English landscape tradition' but noted that 'even in comparatively "straight" paintings Kelly expresses by a wispy group of figures, a dead branch of a tree, a broken gate or a pallid statue, some element of poetry discovered by his imagination rather than his recording eye.' Something of this quality is felt in his Henbury Hall painting.

Read also said: 'Not content with such an obtrusive romantic accent in an otherwise realistic record, he abandons the limits of nature's topography and invents the landscapes of a dream world. The details may be exact – the houses and pedestals, the urn and the wrought-iron: all are actual, as such things are actual in a dream. But their arrangement is poetic: it is – the word cannot be avoided – super-realistic.' Read considered him 'a poet of the inner court'.

Kelly's post-war projects ranged from book illustration to stage design. The latter included sets for Old Vic productions. He provided the illustrations for the *At Home* books by his friend Elizabeth Burton, dealing with the domestic interiors and furnishings of the Elizabethans, Jacobeans, Georgians and early Victorians.

Amanda Harling wrote in 1994: 'Thereafter he painted portraits of the houses of the rich in Britain and in the United States and his work was always in demand. Understandably so, for the mystical, evocative ambience which he bestowed upon these houses was enormously appealing to his discerning clientele. When compared with Kelly's luminous canvases the work of other artists specialising in domestic architecture (with one or two exceptions) pales into pedestrian insignificance.'

Clearly, Felix Kelly established a popularity with the aristocracy and developed a circle of enthusiastic collectors. His life and career is detailed in an enjoyable book by Donald Bassett, called *Fix: The Art and Life of Felix Kelly* (2007). Its author recalled being struck when he first saw Kelly's work by the 'strange power of the pictures – a mix of Surrealism and 18th century style topographical drawing'.

Bassett also suggests that Kelly's introduction to upper-class clients came through the artist Lord Berners, his neighbour Lord Faringdon and Lord Grantley, who introduced him to the Astors and Brownlows. When his country house views were displayed at the Lefevre in 1944, the gallery advertised that they would 'be pleased to accept commissions to paint Country Houses' on Mr Kelly's behalf. It is thought that it was through his high society London circle that he met Sebastian de Ferranti – possibly through an introduction from George Howard.

George Howard was an eager collector – and more – and he described the paintings created for him by Kelly as possessed of a 'heartbreaking nostalgia in their never-never-land appeal'. The nostalgia of his style links him to one of the great literary monuments to the retreat of civilisation, Evelyn Waugh's novel *Brideshead Revisited*.

In 1980, the famously faithful-to-text Granada television adaptation of the novel was filmed at Castle Howard. A couple of years later, Howard decided to spend part of the location fee on murals for his newly created Garden Hall, designed by young architect Julian Bicknell (b.1945) in part of the house that had been damaged in the fire of 1940, which also destroyed the dome. The Garden Hall was finished not as a restoration of the lost interior, but as 'a classical room with something of the feeling of the outdoors or a temple in a park'. Marbled pilasters framed large niches, shaped like windows, with massive keystones inspired by Hawksmoor (who had, of course, been Vanbrugh's more experienced architect-assistant on the design and building of Castle Howard from 1699).

BELOW Felix Kelly's designs for the bridge for the lake (later painted Chinese red) and the entrance gates.

ABOVE The Cave, on the Henbury estate, as re-visualised by Felix Kelly.

The murals painted by Kelly appear as views through the windows of a garden temple, with each view focused on an imaginary tower: Vanbrugh's Belvedere, the Pavilion at Holywell, Totterdown Uphill and Ballyshannon Tower. Each tower is set in a Claudian landscape, with pale blue sky, clouds and hints of dawn or twilight. They were intended to be what the novel's principal character, Charles Ryder (partly based on Rex Whistler and John Piper), might have painted: 'an ivy clad ruin in the foreground, rocks and waterfall affording a rugged introduction to the receding parkland behind' – but Waugh can hardly have imagined these curiously surreal but learned images.

Kelly became a close friend of Howard and a regular guest, spending Christmas with the family on several occasions. Donald Bassett's monograph on the artist notes his 'expat' association with the British aristocracy, observing: 'The closeness of his character to that of Charles Ryder, the artist in Waugh's novel, is obvious; it was like the fulfilment of a prophecy.'

Kelly designed garden buildings for friends from the 1960s. He advised on the restoration of a Gothic summer house at Daylesford, for Lord Rothermere, in 1965; in 1973–78, he helped on the 'Gothicisation' of the Dower House at Cornhill-on-Tweed, enlivening a plain Victorian house. In around 1977–78, after they had been introduced, probably in London, Sebastian de Ferranti involved Kelly in the improvement of houses on the Henbury estate, especially The Cave, which was re-cast in the image of an eighteenth-century romantic eye-catcher or folly.

ABOVE The Cave as executed; in some ways this late-1970s project was a trial run for the designs for the main house.

Sebastian de Ferranti then asked Kelly to help him with the design for a new house on the site of the mansion demolished by his father. Early discussions for the site on which Henbury Hall now stands were, as discussed above, for a single-storey garden pavilion, low and domed, with a room from which to enjoy views across the park. This developed into the idea for a more fully fledged house, with bedrooms on the first floor.

Kelly recalled, in 1988, that they had spent two years (probably 1979–81) developing these ideas before he painted his final oil version: a house modelled on La Rotonda, but with a dome closer to Vanbrugh's diminutive interpretation of Palladio in the Temple of the Four Winds at Castle Howard. This painting was completed in 1981 and exhibited at Partridge's the same year.

As Peter de Figueiredo and Julian Treuherz observed in *Cheshire Country Houses* (1988), 'the idea of starting with a painting and then finding an architect to realise it has a suitably 18th-century ring.' Their description of the painting is worth quoting: 'Kelly's oil painting demonstrated his responsiveness both to the scenic qualities of architecture and the mood of the landscape; a domed Palladian rotunda of warm golden stone and sharply cut classical detail is caught in a theatrical gleam of light against a windswept sky, a storm about to the break and two figures running across a greensward to the house.' It is, as the authors write, and anyone who has seen the painting will agree, 'an enchanting vision'.

Kelly's 'idea' was first given to Quinlan Terry to turn into a set of workable designs informed by Palladian tradition, but after Sebastian de

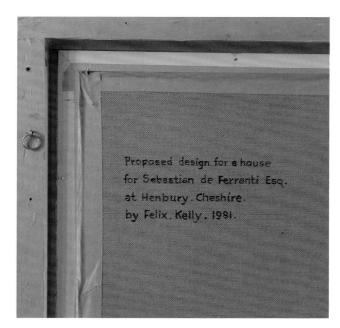

ABOVE LEFT
The Tenants' Hall:
Felix Kelly proposed
a remodelling of the
(mostly nineteenth-
century) windows of the
ground floor into a more
'orangery'-like form.

ABOVE RIGHT On the
reverse of Felix Kelly's
1981 canvas of Henbury
Hall, the neat script of
the artist records that the
painting was indeed 'a
proposed design'.

Ferranti decided that he did not want to continue with Terry, the project was handed over to Julian Bicknell. Letters in the family archive show that Kelly's views held considerable sway with Sebastian de Ferranti, who clearly enjoyed his discussions with the artist. Donald Bassett described the activity of client, artist and architect as similar to the 'committee of taste' at Horace Walpole's Strawberry Hill.

Bicknell and Kelly then were invited to work at Highgrove (Sebastian de Ferranti being a friend of HRH The Prince of Wales, who would later lay the foundation stone at Henbury Hall). Kelly drew up a visual concept for adding distinction to the rather plain 1790s house. A painting was followed by Bicknell's architectural drawings, notably replacing a parapet with a balustrade and adding a central pediment. The proportions were taken from late eighteenth-century models. Bicknell provided a report to the Duchy of Cornwall and, in 1987, the final plans were drawn up by a local architect, Peter Falconer of Stroud, and duly executed.

On completion, Kelly wrote a letter to a friend, Deidre Helmore, which perhaps slightly overstated the extent of the rebuilding, but captures his

RIGHT Felix Kelly's early
sketches for discussion
with Sebastian de Ferranti.

RIGHT Kelly's neo-
Romantic oil painting was
the design proposal, a
reflection of Sebastian de
Ferranti's own vision for a
new house.

excitement and pleasure at working on the project: 'I've redesigned Highgrove in Gloucestershire – their country house – rebuilt in the classic Palladian style and it's had great acclaim in the London press … [the Prince] is thrilled and, naturally, so am I.'

Kelly certainly saw himself as one of the key designers of Henbury Hall. He wrote on 18 April 1988: 'A few years ago I designed a house called Henbury Hall for Sebastian de Ferranti. This was from drawings and, finally, from a painting, of how Mr de Ferranti and I thought that it should look. I am a painter, and not an architect, and Quinlan was called in to carry out the drawings, and the plans, for its construction.' He recounted how Terry was replaced by Julian Bicknell, and observed of the resulting design, 'Whether it is a success – or not – it is what Mr de Ferranti, and I, had envisaged.'

QUINLAN TERRY

By 1981 the stage had been more hopefully set for a new Henbury Hall, domed and porticoed in the spirit of La Rotonda. Kelly was well aware that an architect capable of realising the scheme would need to be involved. Sebastian de Ferranti naturally looked to Quinlan Terry (b.1937), then among a handful of British architects specialising in modern classical architecture.

Terry grew up in Hampstead and was educated at Bryanston and the Architectural Association in London, but firmly rejected the prevailing orthodoxy of Modernism taught in architecture schools, and recalled later: 'In spite of their emphasis on freedom and toleration, the tutors at the AA would not tolerate anyone who questioned their agenda. Modernism was a dogma.'

Terry worked for Sir James Stirling before becoming a pupil and later partner of the renowned classicist Raymond Erith (1904-1973), who designed the Provost's Lodgings at Queen's College Oxford, and remodelled the interiors of 10 Downing Street, and about whom the critic Ian Nairn wrote respectfully: 'a Georgian designer – genuinely Georgian, not "neo".' Terry was a Rome scholar in 1968-69, enjoying a period of first-hand study of classical architecture, which contributed to his determination to design in the classical tradition.

Terry, with Erith, championed the Palladian tradition, and had worked on King's Waldenbury in Hertfordshire for Sir Thomas and Lady Pilkington, and on Waverton in Gloucestershire for Major Jocelyn Hambro. Terry observed of Palladio, in an interview in *Spear's Magazine*, in 2017: 'The reason for his fame is that his genius lay in his humility to copy – yes, yes, copy – Roman buildings 1,500 years before him. The reason for his popularity is that he writes in simple sentences that can be understood by ordinary people.'

David Watkin, author of two recent monographs on Terry, wrote in *Radical Classicism* (2006), 'Quinlan Terry's career began slowly, with minor country buildings from the late 1960s to the late 1970s, but a turning point was Raymond Erith's last commission for a country house, King's Waldenbury, Hertfordshire, for Sir Thomas Pilkington, Bart, in 1968 … Terry understands the human joy in ornament that Modernism has outlawed. His work thus demonstrates the fruits of his realization that Renaissance architects adorned the surface of their building with ornamental forms that were scarcely sanctioned by antiquity.'

Sebastian de Ferranti invited Terry to develop the plans for the house in 1981, and considerable progress was made during that year, with Terry visiting and making a study of La Rotonda. He produced two alternate sets of plans for a house, still named 'The Belvedere' – closely honouring Palladio's La Rotonda – that also contrived to supply the rooms of reception and service that Sebastian de Ferranti saw as appropriate.

These rooms were carefully articulated, with an axial corridor east–west, and a large hall running north–south, and two internal screens of columns creating a dining area under the centre point of the dome. The library and drawing room were located on the west side, and planned to be only 3.6 metres (12 feet) by 5.7 metres (19 feet). Following discussions with Sebastian de Ferranti, and referencing to the plans of *I quattro libri*, Terry evolved the idea of locating the oval staircase hall in one of the northern corners of the plan.

Terry was enthusiastic and his design secured planning permission from the local authority. There was little conflict over the issue with the planners, because of the site and the fact that the earlier house has been demolished, and the house was to be built as the principal house of a small estate – even if the planners reputedly nicknamed the house 'Mr de Ferranti's mausoleum'.

However, in 1982, after long exchanges over certain aspects of the design, Sebastian de Ferranti decided to end his contract with Terry. It seems from the correspondence that the client felt that Terry wanted to work from his own vision of the Palladian ideal and was less eager to follow the neo-Romantic spirit of Kelly's painting. The same correspondence suggests that Sebastian de Ferranti yearned for someone who would be more responsive to his own intensely personal ideas about how the house should look and work.

So, in May 1983, Sebastian de Ferranti wrote to Terry and stated the case:

> I have agonised long and hard over the problem here at Henbury Hall and I have now very, very reluctantly come to the conclusion to try and do it my own way. I am really very, very sorry to have to come to this conclusion and my reasons are manifold and complex but at least one is that the job deserves and demands a very high degree of close association.

JULIAN BICKNELL

And, in May 1983, George Howard and Felix Kelly both encouraged Sebastian de Ferranti to engage Julian Bicknell, who had worked on alterations to the stables at Castle Howard in 1977, the re-creation of the Garden Hall in 1980, and the design of the new library in 1982–83. He was, in many ways, very well placed to take on a new classical project, and it was the beginning of a career which has taken him round the world – designing buildings across the UK and Japan, writing, teaching and being elected Master of the Art Workers' Guild in 2013.

Bicknell recalls:

> My own path to architecture was very influenced by my uncle Peter Bicknell, who taught architecture at Cambridge. He had been at Cambridge in the 1920s, and then the Architectural Association, and worked with George

RIGHT Julian Bicknell,
with the model of
Henbury Hall made by
Richard Armiger.

Grey Wornum on the design of the RIBA building. He designed handsome
Modernist white boxes in the 1930s and the post-war equivalent in the
1950s and 1960s. He was a stalwart of the architecture school and delivered
the history course; my own father was a diplomat so I spent many holidays
with Peter's family in Cambridge. I arrived at King's College, Cambridge,
with the intention of studying engineering in 1963, but moved to architecture within six months. Other students in my year: Spencer de Grey, Robin
Nicholson, John Thompson, Nick Lacey – a lively bunch! Other figures
(tutors) included Sandy Wilson, Leslie Martin, Michael Brawne, Barry
Gasson, and Ted Cullinan. I worked for Ted Cullinan for five years – a long
way from Henbury; his whole approach was very inclusive: 'Do a sketch and
let's see what we think.' David Roberts taught architectural history, and I
attended Pevsner's lectures: very standardised in a large lecture theatre; he
read by rote, his slides used as a kind of catalogue.

Bicknell recalls his 'luck' in securing his first job at Castle Howard. 'George
Howard was a governor of the Royal College of Art and would host fashion
design students for weekends at Castle Howard, and I managed to tag along.'

The first year at Castle Howard was spent on an architectural design project with students from Hugh Casson's department of interior design at the Royal College of Art, a fantasy children's garden with mazes, tree walks and trampolines. Bicknell then became involved in the development of the stables, originally designed by Carr of York, to form a new entrance for the visiting public and the reordering of the costume museum.

> George found out the money to be spent on creating a room [in the house] for the Granada TV *Brideshead* series was going to be £15,000 and just said, let's do it for real. He invited me for a riotous weekend (with Felix Kelly and others) during which we invented the Garden Hall. We had three to four months to get it done, and it was made like a stage set, and the paintings in the end were done after the filming, replacing those done by the scene painters. Felix's paintings are extraordinary – Felix really understood Vanbrugh pictorially like no one else I have ever come across.

Bicknell adds: 'Then Felix rang me up one day and said "Come and meet a friend of mine," but no explanation. I went to his flat, in Prince's Gate, off a rather grand staircase. And I met Sebastian, and within twenty minutes we were all on our hands and knees on the floor looking at the drawings. Sebastian was all enthusiasm. It was the start of a job of three years (and more). I learnt a great deal from looking over Felix's shoulder; he understood things pictorially, but at the same time, when I was given the Henbury commission he did his best to step away and leave me to it.' The curtain had come up on the scene of the relationship which would produce the final design.

LEFT Julian Bicknell's sketch of San Giorgio Maggiore; an illustration in a letter to Sebastian describing a visit to Venice.

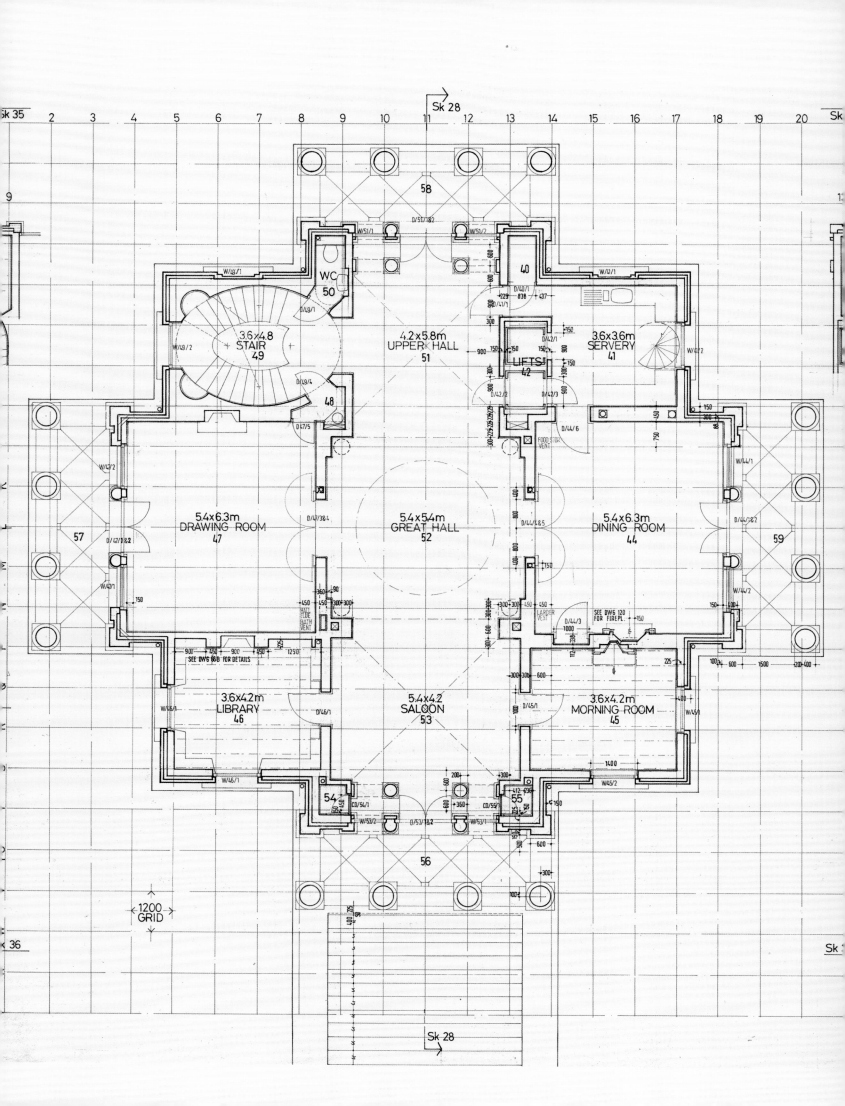

2 3 4 5 6 7 8 9 10 11 12 13 14 15 16 17 18 19 20

58

W/51/1 W/51/1
D/51/1&2

40
D/40/1
W/41/1

W/49/1
WC
50
D/49/1

W/49/2
3.6x4.8
STAIR
49

4.2x5.8m
UPPER HALL
51

SERVERY
41
3.6x3.6m

W/41/2

D/42/1
LIFTS
42

D/42/2

D/42/3

48
D/49/4

D/47/5

FOOD STOR
VENT
D/44/6

57
D/47/1&2

5.4x6.3m
DRAWING ROOM
47

D/47/3&4

5.4x54m
GREAT HALL
52

D/44/4&5

5.4x6.3m
DINING ROOM
44

59
D/44/1&2

W/47/2

W/47/1

W/44/1

W/44/2

HALL
FLUE
BATH
VENT

SEE DWG 66B FOR DETAILS

LARDER
VENT

SEE DWG 120
FOR FIREPL.
D/44/3

3.6x4.2m
LIBRARY
46

W/46/1

D/46/1

5.4x4.2
SALOON
53

D/45/1

3.6x4.2m
MORNING ROOM
45

W/45/1

W/46/1

54
CD/54/1

55
CD/55/1

W/45/2

W/53/2
D/53/1&2
W/53/1

56

1200
GRID

CHAPTER VII

THE FINAL DESIGN

THE FINAL PHASE OF THE DESIGN IS CRITICAL TO THE STORY OF
Henbury Hall. It followed the golden thread of Sebastian de Ferranti's
conviction that Palladio's La Rotonda should be the model for Henbury
Hall – but envisioned with an additional sense of theatre appropriate to the
setting. In May 1983, after that first meeting at Kelly's London flat, the project was placed in the hands of the young Julian Bicknell. Officially taking
charge on 31 May, Bicknell devoted the next three ('or more') years of his
life to the realisation of Sebastian de Ferranti's dream, first in plan and then
in built form.

Bicknell pays homage to Kelly's understanding of architectural impact,
and especially that of the Vanbrughian/Hawksmoorian flavour: 'The columns of the porticoes are closer together than the norm (like Hawksmoor's
mausoleum at Castle Howard); the top floor is clearly compressed in height
as an attic storey with the main cornice crammed up below windows (like
Michelangelo's treatment of St Peter's). The Serliana (Venetian) window
behind each portico is curiously crowded, with the minor columns off centre
from the major ones, and the basement rustication is deliberately oversized.'

Bicknell left Arup Associates in July 1983 and set up his own offices in
Covent Garden. In August, Stern & Woodford were appointed as quantity
surveyors, and model-maker Richard Armiger (an American drawn to the
expertise of architectural model-making in London) was commissioned
to make a scale model, so the design could be better appreciated and discussed. Bicknell had a detailed presentation of drawings ready at the end of
August and in September travelled to Venice, partly on holiday and partly
to make a study of Venetian prototypes, especially of domes and lanterns.
On 24 October the final set of designs was approved.

OPPOSITE A contract
plan of Henbury Hall's
piano nobile illustrating
the final design, including
the slight extension of
the main rooms into the
porticoes, and the scale of
the main central tripartite
hall running north–south.

Interviewed later by Martin Pawley in *The Guardian*, 9 October 1987,
Bicknell observed: 'This new eclecticism stems from the flexible possibili-
ties of machine production and information technology. We know that the
technology is streets ahead of the designers. Technology means you can
choose, and if you can choose, why not classical?' He enjoyed the work
at Henbury Hall, and told Pawley, 'For a start, it's fun. I mean it. It's not
like turning out serviced floorspace for the punters; it's like writing a Bach
fugue. All the elements have a logical relationship that has been going on
for over 2,000 years, so, if you are doing it right, everything fits.'

At the end of his project, he paid homage to his client: 'The client for
Henbury, who probably knows more about Palladio than any architect,
kept spotting things which weren't quite right. He would point to things on
the drawings and I would go away and research them and sure enough they
could be done in another way. There is a kind of intuitive knowledge about
classical building that you can find at all levels from craftsmen to clients.'

Once Bicknell had taken on the project in 1983, he made impressive
strides to resolve this complex project with the client's vision – and that
of Kelly. His major study of La Rotonda, and of the Palladian-inspired
Mereworth Castle, Chiswick Villa and Foot's Cray Place, provided a closer

understanding of English responses to the Palladian model. This gave valuable perspectives from which to rethink Henbury Hall's design within the history of the site. Many threads came together in this phase.

It is key to remember the evolution of the project. It had begun in the spirit of a banqueting house when, in the mid-1970s, John Taylor provided Postmodernist sketches for a single-storey domed building which would make use of the exceptionally fine views. But as plans evolved, and during discussions with Felix Kelly, Sebastian de Ferranti had become more and more convinced that what he wanted to build was actually a house. Finally, in conversation with Kelly, he said: 'Let's put another floor on it.' This was a critical moment in the story of Henbury; from this moment on, it became a dwelling.

But even as a country house proper, it was to remain compact, and this is part of the beauty of the project. Kelly painted his final 'view' of the house, as proposed, in 1981. As a view, it is an opinion and a design, as well as a picture, and Terry evolved his plans broadly in the same spirit. With a close eye on the original model, La Rotonda, he gained permission from the local authority for a house based on these designs to be built. The permitted scheme had four tetrastyle porticoes, a central dome, and the grand central space running north–south on the *piano nobile*.

In the summer of 1983, when Bicknell was appointed architect, he was eager to understand how his client wanted to use and occupy the house. With this in mind, he opined that the rooms on the *piano nobile* (only 3.6 metres – 12 feet – deep on the consented scheme) were too small. They were enlarged to 4.5 metres (15 feet) across. After much thought and discussion with the client, Bicknell then suggested an increase to 5.4 metres (18 feet) in depth for both the drawing room and the dining room; this would subtly project them into the side porticoes on the east and west sides, a variation that has no precedent in Palladio's work.

Adding substantially to the principal rooms of reception, without affecting the overall proportions of the whole, was a decision that made the house. The final plan of the *piano nobile* was resolved into a large, transverse central hall running from north to south, 16.8 metres (56 feet) long, and

BELOW Demonstration sketches illustrating proportional systems, including, on the right, the 'golden rectangle'.

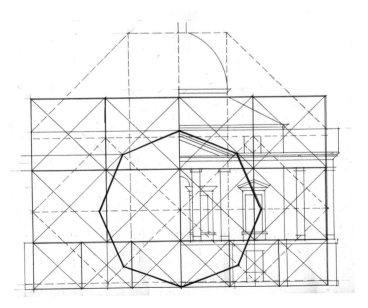

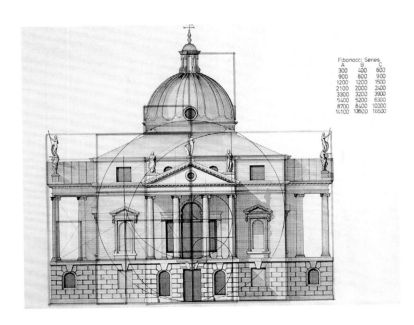

with no division provided by a central screen of columns. This opened the room up to connect with the space under the dome and the circular gallery, giving access to the two interconnected master bedroom suites.

On the *piano nobile*, the rooms have ceilings that are 5.4 metres (18 feet) high, giving an immediate feeling of generosity of space that is echoed in immensely tall, round-headed door cases – and in the tall central window of the Serliana (Venetian) windows to north and south. Bicknell's decision to move the screen of columns to be part of the main opening north and south added a remarkable flavour to the central room, making it appear almost afloat in the landscape that surrounds the house.

Bicknell credits Kelly with the vision for the ground-level entrance hall: 'A baroque effect of the Doric order making an oval within the square geometry of the whole; the cornice is compressed by omitting the frieze, which adds to the feeling of weight above.'

The oval-plan staircase was designed to occupy the north-west corner of the main 'cube' of the house, and it required considerable ingenuity to work with the different height levels through three storeys (the detailed designs for this were finally resolved in July and August 1983). The serving room (with butler's pantry in a mezzanine above) occupies the north-east corner of the *piano nobile*, with a passenger lift which rises the whole three storeys and, behind it, a service lift connecting the kitchen on the ground floor with the servery and the butler's pantry.

After much investigation, including the creation of a number of timber models to study the effect of different profiles, Bicknell essentially followed the model of the dome at Mereworth Castle, with a low, pyramidal roof supporting a dome sitting on a drum. The profile of the dome channelled

BELOW A design which incorporated Kelly's vision for the Tenants' Hall, which was dropped after opposition from local planners.

HENBURY ROTONDA & TENANTS HALL
SOUTH ELEVATIONS

Julian Bicknell ~ Architect
20 Bedford Street
London WC2E 9PH
Telephone: 01-836 5825

Scale: 1:100
Date: 2/10/84   Dwn: JP
Dwg. No.: 207

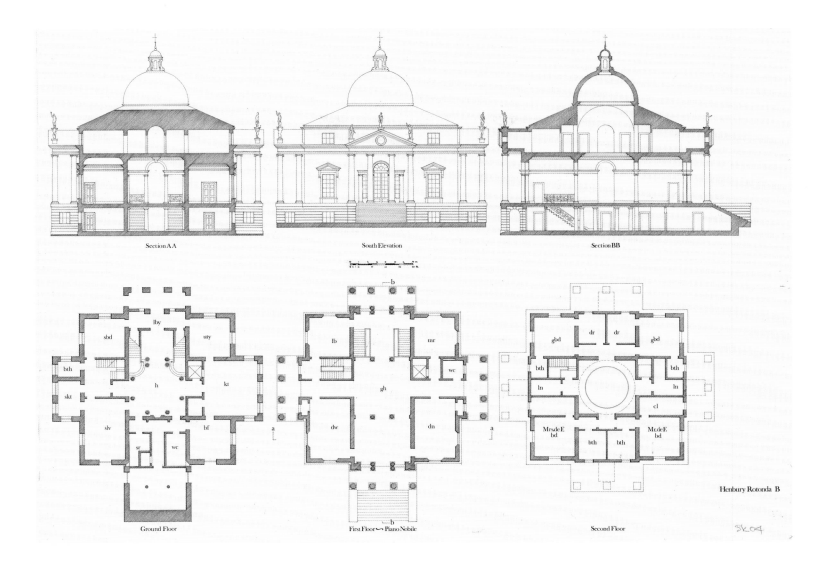

Section A A	South Elevation	Section BB

Henbury Rotonda B

Ground Floor	First Floor ~ Piano Nobile	Second Floor

the Vanbrugh spirit, being more evocative of the ovoid domes of baroque Rome than the perfect hemisphere which appears in Palladio's *I quattro libri* (which Sebastian de Ferranti thought looked uncomfortably like a *chapeau melon* – a bowler hat).

Bicknell was asked to adjust the second floor so it would provide two guest suites in addition to the originally proposed two master suites. Bicknell recalls that it took a lot of work to get four bedrooms – expanding to six when the dressing rooms double up as single rooms – and six bathrooms into the first floor. This was a late change to the project in the summer of 1984, and he took inspiration from the 1890s English 'Free School' and the plans of Voysey and Norman Shaw. He recalls that he amalgamated 'Palladian elegance with comfort and ingenuity' and 'later realised that Lutyens was also doing this to the power of ten'. It was at this point that Bicknell conceived of making incisions into the roofs of the porticoes to create lightwells that would bring daylight into the dressing rooms.

Alongside four double bedrooms and the option of two singles, the estate retained the bedroom and bathroom suites of the converted late seventeenth-century stables known as the Tenants' Hall. This meant that, should the number of guests swell, the two buildings between them could accommodate a sizeable house party. There had been an idea to remodel the Tenants' Hall, replacing the mostly nineteenth-century windows with taller openings, which would have created the effect of an orangery.

ABOVE Earlier iterations of the design shown in plan and section form.

FOLLOWING PAGES An earlier plan showing a different treatment of the staircase, which would have reduced the space of the central hall on the *piano nobile*.

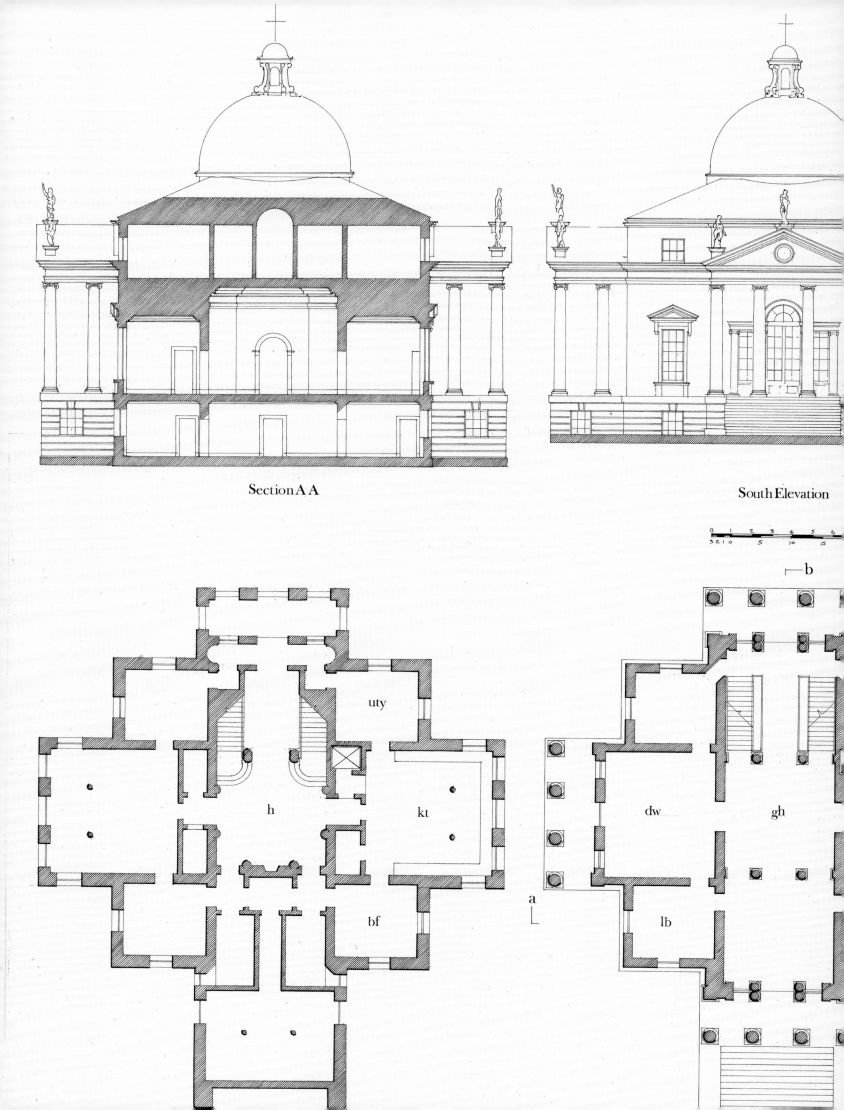

Section A A

South Elevation

uty

h

kt

bf

dw

gh

lb

a

b

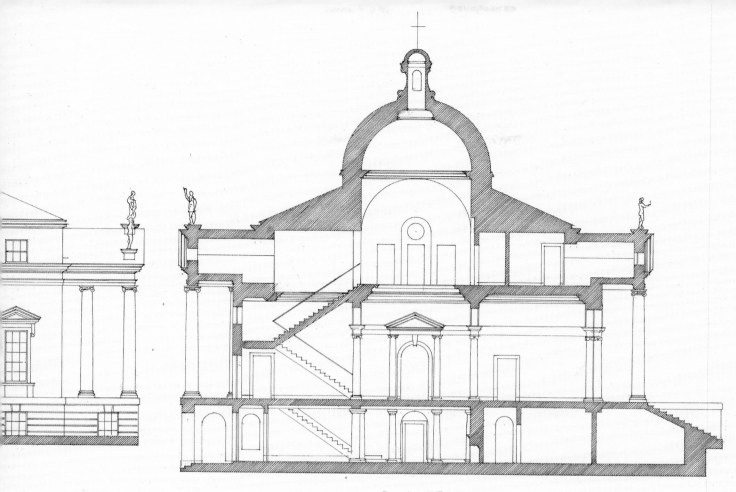

Section BB

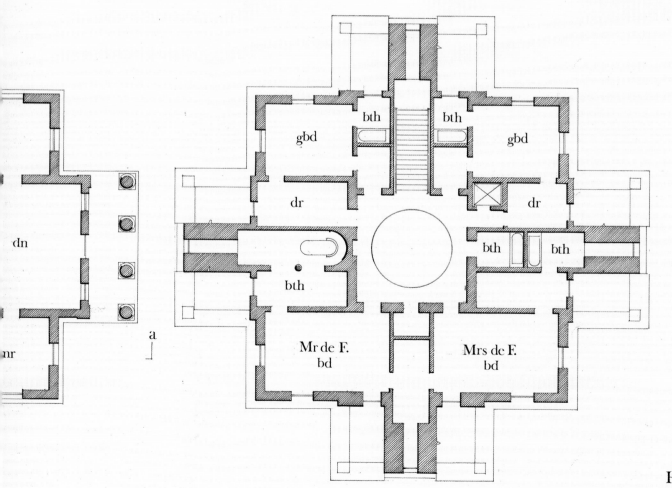

bth   bth

gbd   gbd

dr   dr

dn   bth   bth

bth

nr

a

Mr de F.   Mrs de F.
bd   bd

1:100

Henbury Rotonda C

Kelly provided one of his 'views' and Bicknell drew up plans, but the stables, regardless of their nineteenth-century alterations and post-war conversion, were listed. The estate was advised permission would not be forthcoming, so the plan was shelved.

The proportions of Henbury Hall are particularly admired by people who know the house, both in terms of instinctive reactions to the effect of shapes and masses, and, more objectively, in the scientific underpinning of the design in mathematical formulae. In 2018, Bicknell recalls: 'In designing Henbury, I worked from the basic principles of modular planning laid out by Vitruvius and all subsequent authorities – the use of a module derived from the column diameter.' This, needless to say, was the essential approach of Palladio, the module system ensuring that every component is expressed as a fraction or multiple of the singular module. Palladio most often used two Vicentine feet as his column diameter and wall thickness.

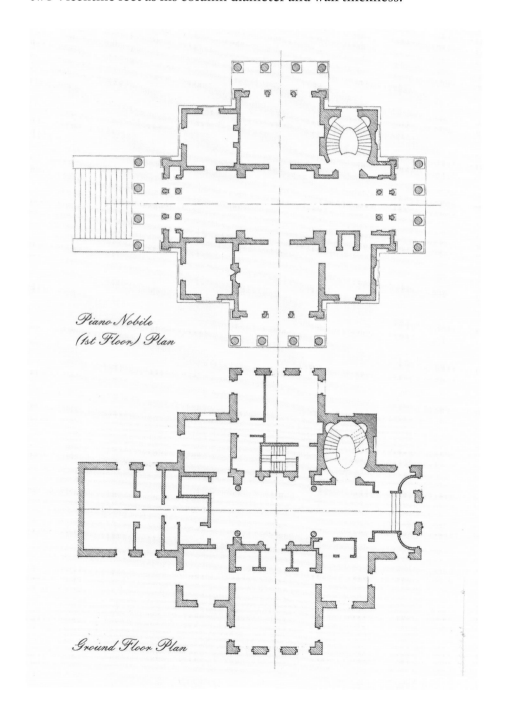

Piano Nobile (1st Floor) Plan

Ground Floor Plan

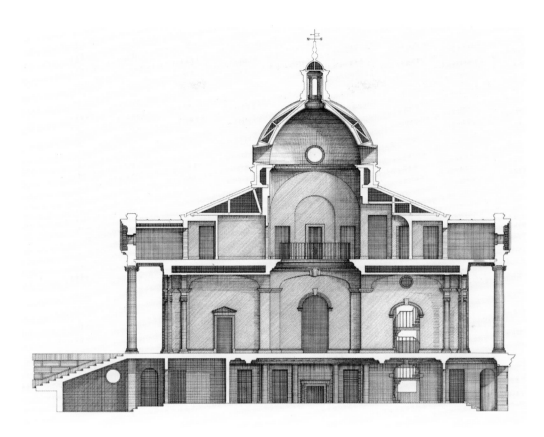

At Henbury Hall, the module was established by the diameter of the principal Ionic column – 60 centimetres (2 feet). The height of the column (and the ceiling of the *piano nobile*) is nine modules – 5.4 metres (18 feet). The secondary order, three-fifths of the principal order, is expressed in the Venetian windows behind the porticoes, and so on through all the components and spaces of the house.

Bicknell says: 'In the early 1980s, I had had no formal instruction in the classical orders and very little first-hand experience. However, that little experience hadeen with buildings of impeccable pedigree – the stable buildings of Castle Howard, by John Carr of York; and Castle Howard itself, by Vanbrugh and Hawksmoor, where I designed new interiors for the Garden Hall and Library.'

In the light of how it prepared him for the work at Henbury Hall, this experience was particularly useful. 'Although the work on the stables was not overtly classical, it required us to make an accurate and detailed survey, in the course of which we learned that, in his design, Carr uses a very limited array of standard dimensions, mostly simple multiples or fractions of a foot, all of them closely related to each other.' This experience, and the work on the main house, was formative for Bicknell, and critical to his work on Henbury Hall in giving first-hand experience of the proportional systems in use in the eighteenth century.

Bicknell recalls: 'The work in the Garden Hall at Castle Howard was my first exercise in the classical vocabulary. I was expecting a system of standard dimensions that I would have to understand if my interior was to work with the established geometry of the building.'

It took a while puzzling over the survey drawings of the fire-gutted rooms to work it out, but what finally emerged proved remarkably simple.

BELOW AND OPPOSITE
Things fall into place: the
north entrance elevation
and a section of the near-
final design for Henbury
Hall by Julian Bicknell.

Everything in the house is related to a module of 10 inches. The stone
paving in the Great Hall is laid out on a 20-inch grid (two modules); the
pilasters of the hall are 30 inches across (three modules); the door openings
are 50 inches wide (five modules); the ceilings of the state rooms are 140
inches high (fourteen modules); and so on. Thus we used the same module
for our new interiors. The pilasters in the new Garden Hall are 20 inches
wide (two modules) and all the other features set out on a related grid –
the paving pattern repeating the 20-inch grid of the rest of the house. …
The new library interior was similarly regulated, using a 10-inch-wide
pilaster, and setting out a grid for the bookcases and all the other features
of the room.

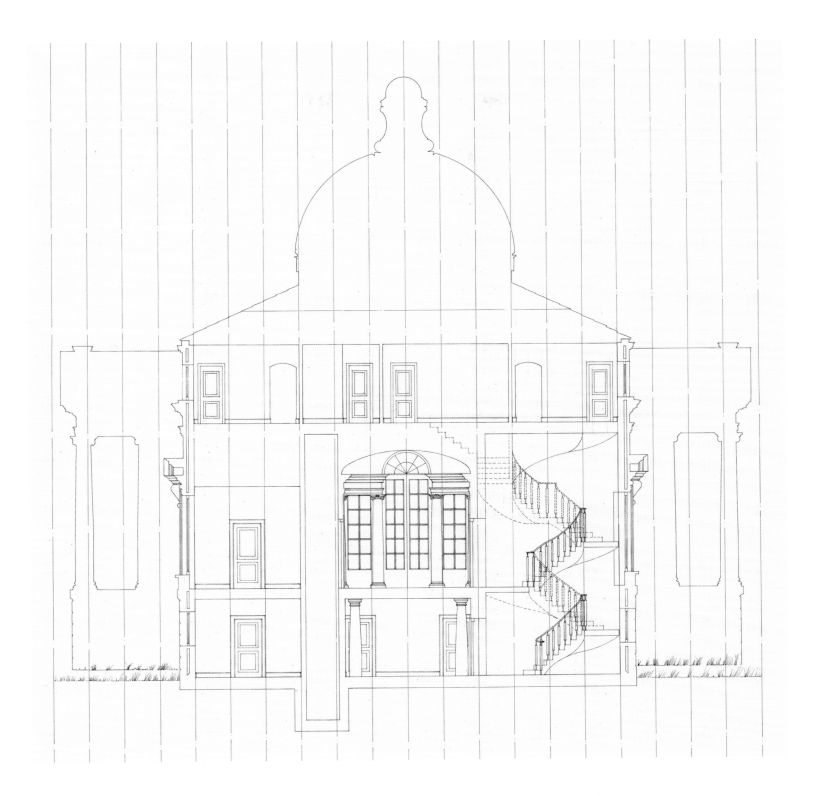

So when it came to the design of Henbury Hall, Bicknell naturally began at once to look 'for a similar co-ordinating system of modular dimensions. As it happens, my first experiments with a column diameter of sixty centimetres, the metric equivalent of two feet – which seemed a simple way to start – proved very successful and remained the basis of the design.'

Thus there is an overarching proportional relationship governing the whole design. Bicknell writes: 'The plans at each floor are laid out on a grid of 1.2 metres – i.e., two column diameters. Each of the four porticoes is 7.2 metres – twelve diameters; the windows are 1.2 metres wide – two diameters; the central hall is 5.4 × 5.4 × 5.4 metres, or nine diameters cubed;

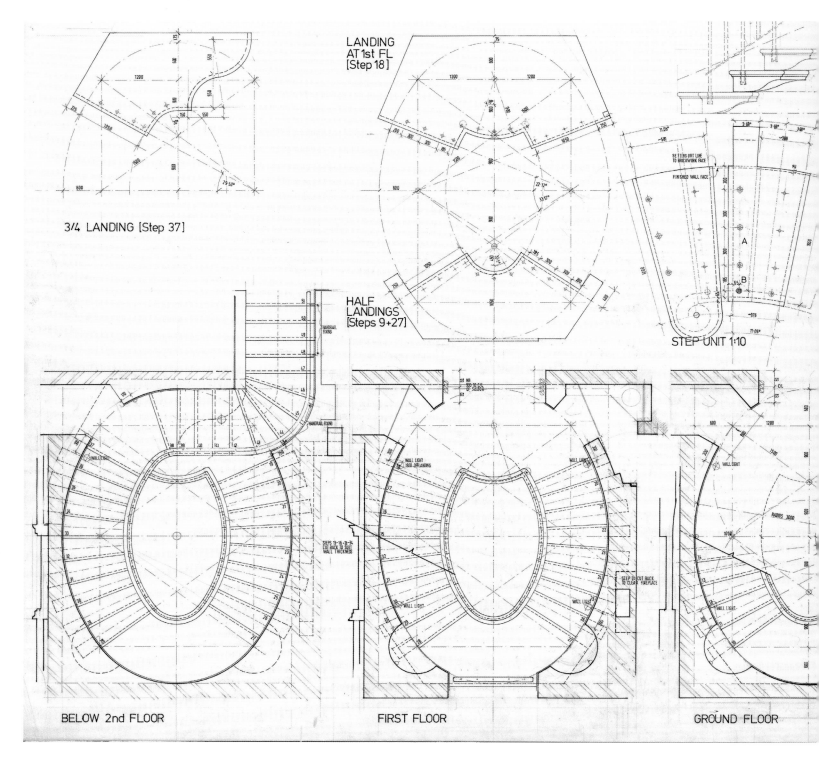

3/4 LANDING [Step 37]

LANDING AT 1st FL [Step 18]

HALF LANDINGS [Steps 9+27]

STEP UNIT 1:10

BELOW 2nd FLOOR

FIRST FLOOR

GROUND FLOOR

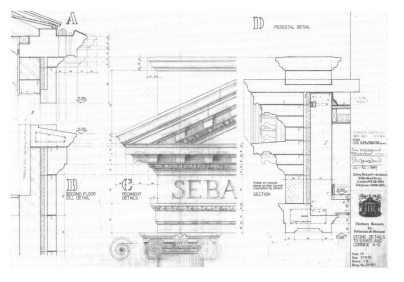

A

B
SECOND FLOOR CILL DETAIL

C
PEDIMENT DETAILS

D
PEDESTAL DETAIL

SECTION

SEBA

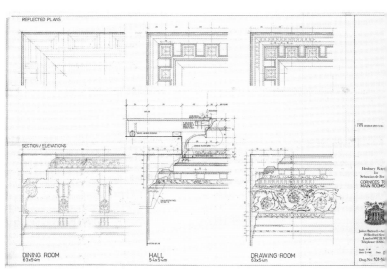

REFLECTED PLANS

SECTION / ELEVATIONS

DINING ROOM

HALL

DRAWING ROOM

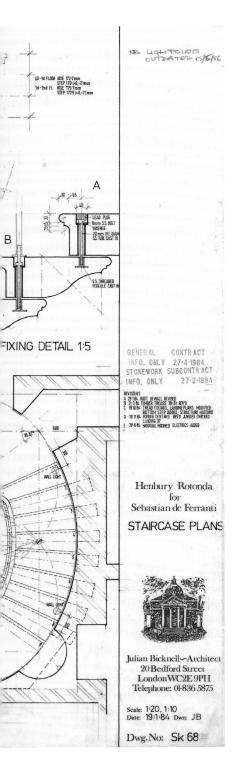

FIXING DETAIL 1:5

GENERAL CONTRACT
INFO. ONLY 27·4·1984
STONEWORK SUBCONTRACT
INFO. ONLY 27·2·1984

Henbury Rotonda
for
Sebastian de Ferranti

STAIRCASE PLANS

Julian Bicknell~Architect
20 Bedford Street
London WC2E 9PH
Telephone: 01-836 5875

Scale: 1:20, 1:10
Date: 19·1·84 Dwn: JB

Dwg.No: Sk 68

Working drawings of the
cantilevered staircase, cupola
and door cases.

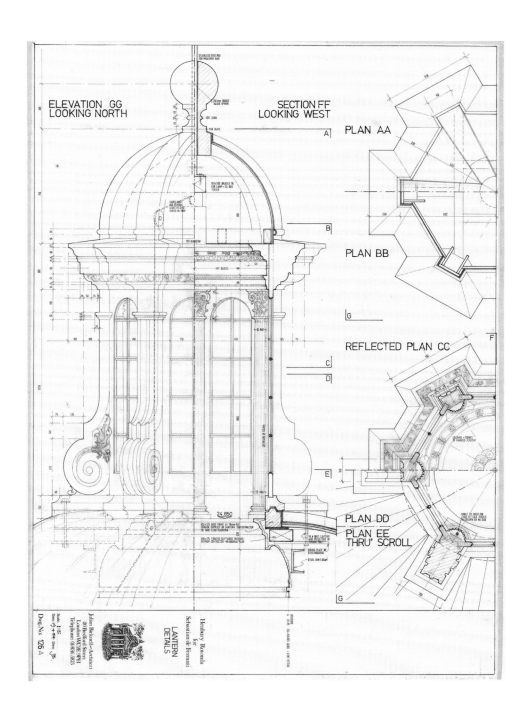

ELEVATION GG
LOOKING NORTH

SECTION FF
LOOKING WEST

PLAN AA

PLAN BB

REFLECTED PLAN CC

PLAN DD
PLAN EE
THRU' SCROLL

Henbury Rotonda
for
Sebastian de Ferranti

LANTERN
DETAILS

Julian Bicknell~Architect
20 Bedford Street
London WC2E 9PH
Telephone: 01-836 5875

Dwg.No: 126 A

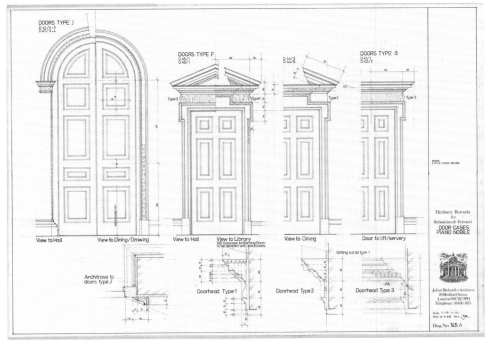

DOORS TYPE J

DOORS TYPE F

DOORS TYPE G

View to Hall

View to Dining/Drawing

View to Hall

View to Library

View to Dining

Door to lift/servery

Architrave to
doors type J

Doorhead Type 1

Doorhead Type 2

Doorhead Type 3

Henbury Rotonda
for
Sebastian de Ferranti

DOOR CASES
PIANO NOBILE

Julian Bicknell~Architect
20 Bedford Street
London WC2E 9PH
Telephone: 01-836 5875

Dwg.No: 145 A

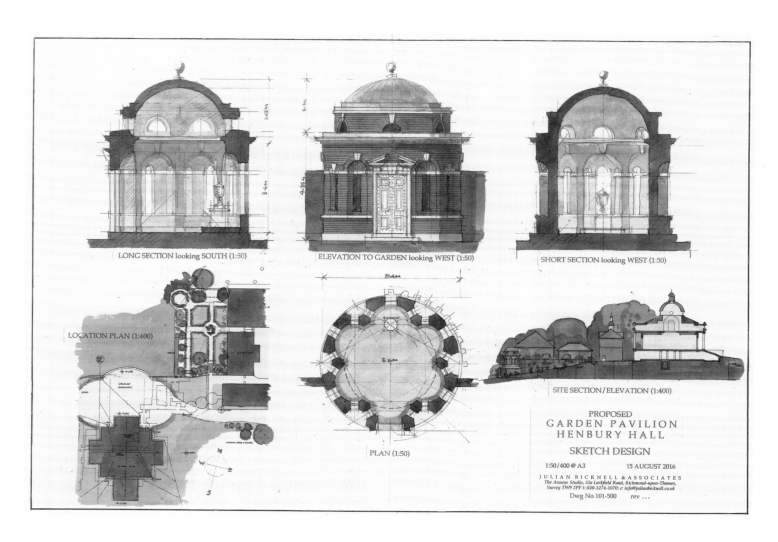

LONG SECTION looking SOUTH (1:50)

ELEVATION TO GARDEN looking WEST (1:50)

SHORT SECTION looking WEST (1:50)

LOCATION PLAN (1:400)

PLAN (1:50)

SITE SECTION / ELEVATION (1:400)

PROPOSED
GARDEN PAVILION
HENBURY HALL

SKETCH DESIGN

1:50 / 400 @ A3   15 AUGUST 2016

JULIAN BICKNELL & ASSOCIATES
The Annexe Studio, 32a Larkfield Road, Richmond-upon-Thames,
Surrey TW9 2PF t: 020-3274-1070: e: info@julianbicknell.co.uk

Dwg No 101-500   rev ...

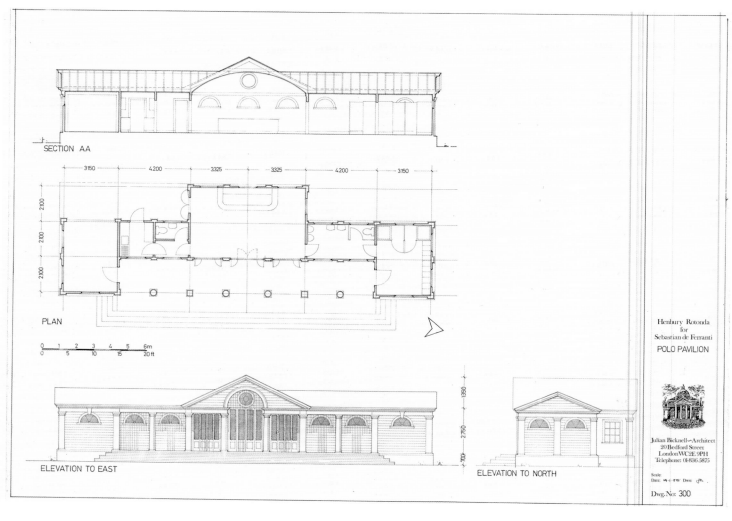

SECTION AA

PLAN

ELEVATION TO EAST

ELEVATION TO NORTH

Henbury Rotonda
for
Sebastian de Ferranti

POLO PAVILION

Julian Bicknell ~ Architect
20 Bedford Street
London WC2E 9PH
Telephone: 01-836.5875

Dwg. No: 300

the reception rooms are 5.4 × 6.3 metres, nine by ten-and-a-half diameters; the corner rooms 3.6 × 4.3 metres, six by seven diameters.'

For Henbury's interior detail, Bicknell recalls that he looked to the richness of the world of Georgian domestic architecture and the plentiful publications used by designers and craftsmen of that era: 'In developing the detail of the orders – the setting out of bases, capitals and *entasis* of the columns, of the entablatures, window surrounds, cornices, etc. – I used the standard early eighteenth-century pattern books, in particular James Gibbs's *Rules for Drawing the Several Parts of Architecture* (1732), and Batty Langley's *The Builder's Jewel* (1741) – both based on a system of simply understood geometric ratios, rather than Palladio's rather cumbrous arithmetic system of modules and minutes. Thus, the main columns are 5.4 metres (nine diameters) high; the main entablature is 1.05 metres (one and three-quarters diameters); the brackets supporting the cornice are at 0.3 metres (half a diameter) centres.'

On the proportion of rooms, Bicknell further notes:

In developing the overall size and height, I was always looking for simple ways of relating width to height. The simplest method is to make height and width the same – defining the setting out of various features by a series of squares and/or circles. I also used a series of 'preferred dimensions' – the successive terms of a Fibonacci series based on the column diameter: 0.3 metres (half a diameter), 0.9 metre (one and a half diameters), 1.2 metres (two diameters), 2.1 metres (three and a half diameters); 3.3 metres (five and a half diameters), 5.4 metres (nine diameters), etc. Each term of a Fibonacci series is defined as the sum of the previous two. Each successive pair of terms has the intriguing property that they approach the golden ratio (1.618:1) – defined as 'the lesser is to the greater as the greater is to the whole.'

So-called Golden Rectangles, using this ratio for their length and breadth, have a further interesting property – that if a perfect square is drawn on the shorter side, the remaining rectangle is also a Golden Rectangle. So, using a sequence of preferred dimensions derived from a Fibonacci series makes a design in which all of whose features are closely related to each other – both through the use of a modular grid of squares, and through the repetition of related Golden Rectangles. For example, the columns of the minor order that frames the Serliana within each portico, and appears internally at each end of the Great Hall, are 3.3 metres high – compared with the 5.4 metres of the major order – a near-perfect golden ratio.

The success of the design of Henbury Hall owes a great deal to Bicknell's balancing Kelly's intuitive approach to proportion with his own more scientific discipline – the result a rare harmony of parts. Small details and subtle planning are as much a part of its overall impact as the impression conveyed by its exterior on first – and subsequent – viewings. The rigour of its proportions creates an extraordinary sensory stimulation as you pass through its rooms, as you rise up the cantilevered staircase, and enter the enjoyable and dizzying volume of the central hall and dome void.

Back in October 1984, all this was still on the drawing board, and the physical creation was just about to begin.

OPPOSITE ABOVE AND BELOW Julian Bicknell's design for a pavilion, or mausoleum, to adjoin the enclosed garden on the north side of the house, was never executed. Nor was the elegant polo pavilion also designed by Julian Bicknell.

CHAPTER VIII
BUILDING THE HOUSE

IT IS ONE THING TO DESIGN A DREAM HOUSE, QUITE ANOTHER to build it. This requires the most careful and exacting preparation, including the appointment of reliable contractors and the co-ordination and management of the entire process. After Tarmac Cubitts (originally Cubitts and later Tarmac Construction) had been appointed as the main building contractors, work at Henbury began on 13 September 1984. The foundations were blessed by the then (Roman Catholic) Bishop of Shrewsbury, Joseph Gray. The work was finally completed two years and nine months later in March 1987 – Bicknell calculating there were '200 man years of work in the Henbury Rotonda'.

The designing and planning had been prepared well in advance, with Julian Bicknell and his team (Gerry Cahill, Kevin Rowbotham, Jenny Playle, Chris Hay, Martin Herman, Sean Dockry, Steve Chapman and others) providing a full set of working drawings in July 1984, supported by detailed drawings from Bob Dwyer, the services consultant, and Stephen Revess, the structural engineer. But plans are only as good as the men on the ground supervising them, and crucially for the smooth running of the project, John McLaughlin was appointed Tarmac's principal site agent.

Looking back in 2018, Julian Bicknell recalls: 'John was brought out of retirement to run the project. He smoked an obnoxious pipe, but he really understood the business of coordination. He would take me aside after the formal site meetings and suggest solutions to problems – whether architectural, contractual or diplomatic.'

As planned, the new house was built precisely in the middle of the site of the old house, located above the old brick-vaulted cellars. This was a double challenge. In order to make the new building totally sound, it was

ABOVE, LEFT TO RIGHT Photographs taken in 1984–85 showing: the works to strengthen the old cellars; the quarry in France from which the stone derives; the building up of the ashlar; the stone awaiting use on site; the view from within the brick shell.

decided not to use the old cellars as the foundations, so the house was designed to carefully straddle these by means of short bore piles extending below the cellar floor and a thick concrete slab above the cellar vaults, secure and strong enough to take the weight of the new structure above – devised especially by Revess, the structural engineer. The old cellars, surviving from the original house, extend some distance beyond the new building to both east and west – a maze of passages and chambers. On the west, the magnificent vaulted undercroft of the late seventeenth-century house was preserved and renovated as a wine cellar.

As Bicknell recalls: 'On the east the passages reached a door into the Little Garden. Some of the cellars under the new building had already collapsed. A few others were filled in, but enough survived to make a continuous passage connecting the wine cellars to a new stair up into the new house and the service lift connecting to the ground floor utility room and the butler's pantry on the *piano nobile*. The passage through to the Little Garden was preserved and the cellars extended eastwards to provide a new boiler room and underground connection to the Tenants' Hall.'

The walls of the house were built in load-bearing brick with concrete floors. The decision to face the new building in stone was one of the boldest of the whole project, and the external stonework was the responsibility of William Anelay's of York, a firm founded in 1747 and managed by Peter Johnson (who recalls, in 2018, 'It was relatively straightforward from a fixing point of view, but we had to work closely with Tarmac about scaffolding and hoisting. It was a challenge to keep enough masons on site.') Palladio's La Rotonda, like most of the villas he designed in the Veneto, was faced in stucco with stone columns, window surrounds and trim, and this is also the case with later neo-Palladian houses built in Britain, such as Colen Campbell's Mereworth Castle. But at Henbury, architect and client had resolved early on that stucco would not be the best aesthetic – or, indeed, practical – proposition in the notoriously damp climate of north-west England. Bicknell observes: 'I think Felix's vision was certainly envisaged in stone. He would have liked the effects of time and weather.'

Sebastian de Ferranti wanted the stone to have a degree of warmth and, after much discussion, the favoured choice was a buff-coloured oolitic limestone, similar to Clipsham stone. Bicknell and de Ferranti went to look at the restoration of Magdalen Tower, in Oxford, and expected to be in favour of the native English stone used there. However, they ended up choosing a French limestone from Bravilliers, near Nancy, in north-east France – which was cheaper and could also be delivered more reliably.

In a memorandum to Sebastian de Ferranti, dated 22 October 1984, Bicknell noted: 'The Euville stone proposed for the plinth and first-floor band course is not liked even in the sand-coloured version. A warm Savonnière would be preferred.' Savonnière (a generic term for the stone produced by three working quarries in the commune of that name) is an oolitic and shelly limestone from the Upper Jurassic, Portlandian stratum. The colour range is famously broad, from 'blonde' to grey, and the stone is renowned for its resistance to frost. Cathedral Works at Chichester, sole agent for Rocamat, which was the largest supplier of French stone to England at the time, organised the cutting and shipping from France.

Bicknell recalls in 2018: 'The agent was a good salesman and a bon viveur. He arranged a three-day trip across Northern France visiting the various quarries and workshops. I remember being hugely impressed by the scale of the French quarries with cliffs of perfect stone thirty feet high, a plethora of large scale machinery and workmen working extensively with compressed air tools – a marked contrast to the equivalent in the UK where stone beds rarely exceed ten feet in height and most masonry was then still finished by hand. The trip was also organised to explore the best of the local cuisine and wines.'

Natural stone was used for the wall facings, columns and steps, following full-scale drawings by Bicknell, and the decorative stonework details were cast in high-quality artificial stone by a specialist company, Broadmead of Maidstone, from models carved in limewood by Dick Reid of York. The natural stone was cut and worked at the quarry itself, then delivered to site, all cut and dressed and beautifully shrinkwrapped – ready to be put together by Anelay's on site. However, there were delays caused by the exceptionally cold winter of 1984–85, which affected work both in the quarries in France and on site in Cheshire. On 9 May 1985, M. D. Arbanere, of Rocamat Ltd, wrote to apologise for the delays, quoting 'les fortes intempéries de l'hiver qui ont bousculé nos programmes de production'.

The bitter cold of that winter has become part of the legend of the house. When he came to lay the foundation stone on a chilly winter evening in February, HRH The Prince of Wales tapped it smartly the traditional three times with a wooden mallet, and the stone was so cold that he chipped off the corner. Harry Jocelyn, Professor of Classics at the University of Manchester, composed a suitable Latin motto to commemorate the event: 'LAPIDEM PRIMVM HENBVRII CAROLVS PRINCEPS WALLIAE MCMLXXXV POSVIT AC FREGIT', which in modern English is, 'This first stone of Henbury was laid – and broken – by Charles, Prince of Wales, 1985.'

Bicknell recalls in 2018: 'It was an extraordinary moment when we put up the scaffolding and realised just quite how good the view was going to be.' Similar emotions were felt as the brick shell began to come together. The team aimed to complete the shell and cover the building as quickly as possible so as to make it weathertight before the next winter, to allow works to continue within. By April 1985, the brickwork outer shell had reached first-floor level and by August it had been finished as far as the base of the dome, while the stone facing had reached the first floor. Photographs of the building rising in stages give an uncanny feeling of grandeur and dignity, imparted by the quality of the core design – even when shrouded in scaffolding.

By the end of August 1985, the steel frame of the dome, again devised by structural engineer Revess, and made by L. B. Structures of Wolverhampton, was in place. This was another novel solution, in essence an octagonal steel frame bolted to a concrete collar. Plywood ribs were cut to the profile of the dome and fitted to the frame. Tarmac's joiners then covered the steel skeleton with boards, bent over the framing rather in the manner of a

BELOW, LEFT TO RIGHT The brick shell; the rising stonework; the columns of the porticoes; the shell of the dome; the dome finally clad. Even in scaffolding the dramatic impression of this new building was self-evident.

boat. This was then covered in lead (by H.E. Simm & Son of Liverpool).

The effectiveness of the design had a positive effect on the programme: on 17 September 1985, Bicknell wrote to Sebastian de Ferranti: 'Progress on the dome is satisfactory. In fact the steel cage proved simpler than feared so that delays on the concrete ring beam have been recovered and the timber-work to the dome started a little ahead of schedule.' Bicknell also prepared full-scale drawings for the detailing of the external leadwork, the bull's-eye windows and the timber elements over which it was fitted. This followed the example of the leadwork on the dome at Mereworth Castle.

By 12 December 1985, Bicknell was able to report: 'It seems that the stonework is now flowing freely and 90 per cent of the walling to eaves level should be complete by Christmas. Window frames are due to arrive any day so that a watertight building is not far off. The stonework to the porticoes will continue into the New Year. The pediments include the most ticklish castings and cannot be rushed. I do hope we do not have any further hiccups because it will soon be vital to keep rainwater off the porticoes too if the rooms below are to be kept dry.' He must have wondered how often Palladio had to deal with extreme freezing conditions and incessant rain.

They were also moving forward with the interiors at this time, and he wrote of the stone floors: 'It seems we have got the right pattern now. I am assembling samples of decorative stones for the borders, etc., including varieties of Purbeck Marble. I like the notion that the stone of the floor should be from English sources and there are some very rich examples to choose from.' Elaborate boilers were installed by Longworth & Sons and electrical installation was by G. Priestwall & Son of Stockport. Ironmongery was by Thews of Liverpool.

During the summer of 1985, Dr Dick Reid, the famed York woodcarver, with whom Julian Bicknell had worked closely at Castle Howard, became involved in the external detailing of the stonework. Born in Newcastle upon Tyne in 1934, Dick Reid served an apprenticeship as an Architectural Wood and Stone Carver in the studio of Ralph Hedley (Craftsmen) Ltd of

Newcastle, and attended Durham University Art School. After a period as an army officer, he set up a woodcarving and stonemasonry workshop in York, establishing himself as an expert on restoration and conservation, contributing to new-build schemes both nationally and internationally, providing church monuments across the country, and training many of the best carvers at work today (he was elected Master of the Art Workers' Guild for 2005).

His strength lay not only in his knowledge but also in his skills as a hands-on woodcarver, stonemason and sculptor. Bicknell recalls: 'I would do an outline design for a detail and Dick would say, "You mean like this?" We worked well together.' Reid in turn recalls, 'Everyone who worked on Henbury Hall enjoyed it, and I think Julian's charm and enthusiasm helped keep everything on track.'

Reid's work in the restoration of Spencer House, in St James's, in the late 1980s, where he had overall stylistic control of ornament while working for Lord Rothschild, was one of the pinnacles of his publicly recognised achievement. This work overlapped with his work at Henbury. From 1989 Reid was a trustee (along with Bicknell) of HRH the Prince of the Wales's Institute of Architecture. Bicknell was grateful for the confidence and knowledge Reid brought to Henbury, for the quality and detail of cast stonework and the carved wood details within. This is evidenced in Reid's highly finished carved wooden architraves for the tall door cases prepared by Robert Dent of York – Bicknell and Reid together identified the model of scrolled leaf carved detail found in Beningbrough Hall in Yorkshire (work which could be hand-carved at a rate of about six inches a day).

Reid produced the timber matrices from which the moulds for the cast stonework elements, such as the Ionic capitals, were made. Bicknell recalls:

'The capitals were made up in clay and we had a jolly day in Dick's shop re-forming the volutes to project in a more baroque fashion, reversing the leaf that covers the junction between the volute and egg-and-dart, and replacing the traditional floret by the Ferranti lily.' Reid also produced the console brackets (the latter carved and moulded with one detachable part to give the full scroll effect); rubber moulds were then made up by Broadmead.

The capitals were built up in clay in Reid's York workshop, with the help of assistants Charles Gurrey, Martin Dutton and Matthew Hyde, and then carved in an imported Russian Baltic pine, chosen for its denseness and suitability for carving. Dick Reid's wife, 'Buff', recalls in 2018 that some of the carving for Henbury Hall was done by Martin Dutton, the workshop's principal carver at the time, 'a fabulous carver and a great example of what a disabled person can achieve if given the opportunity to train for a craft. He was profoundly deaf & dumb, & a lovely man. He trained with "Mousey" Thompson.'

The lantern was one of Reid's many contributions and coordinated the manufacture and assembly with colleagues in York, contributing the scrolled buttresses and heavily decorated cornice himself. The entire construction was delivered whole and was lifted on to the dome by a 24-metre (80-foot) crane. Nine feet (2.7 metres) high – without the weathervane – it also weighs half a ton. The diminutive Corinthian columns of the lantern make a lighthearted comment on the classical tradition, part of the stately progress of the orders throughout the house, following Doric in the basement storey and Ionic on the *piano nobile*.

Bicknell suggested introducing the lily and ring, based on the heraldic device of Sebastian de Ferranti's Ziani ancestors, as a motif to be used in a number of places, starting with the column capitals. This notion was warmly welcomed by Sebastian de Ferranti, and the heraldic allusion was used as a form of architectural decoration elsewhere in the house.

LEFT The arrival of the cupola; Dick Reid helped evolve the design with Julian Bicknell.

RIGHT Interior details, including the capitals of the north and south window screens, were all produced from matrices prepared by Dick Reid.

It appears, for example, on the keystone of the south-facing window and the top of the arched architraves to the dining room and drawing room (Sebastian's Ziani ancestors had been doges of Venice, and the ring is an iconographic combination derived from the doge's annual service of Venice's marriage to the sea.)

The same motif was also employed on the weathervane, and Bicknell wrote on 17 September 1985: 'The drawing is modelled very closely on St Martin-in-the-Fields. It is a pierced metal sheet, and the notion is to use the lily and the ring as the pierced pattern. The whole thing is gilded for longevity.' The weathervane was made by F. Tomlinson & Son, of Stockport, and placing it *in situ* was an enormous challenge, as the scaffolding reached only to the base of the lantern, and for a time they despaired of getting the vane in place within the single day that the big crane was on site. Bicknell recalls: 'In the end we did manage, with three of us supporting each other like a Catalan human pyramid to guide it into place.'

Bicknell looks back with special pleasure on the design and construction of the main staircase:

> The main stair is a so-called cantilever spiral stair set out on an oval plan. Each tread is a single precast element locked into the enclosing wall and supported by the treads below – an ingenious piece of engineering first deployed in England by Inigo Jones at the Queen's House in Greenwich. The oval setting out at Henbury uses an arrangement of four circular arcs that means every tread is the same shape and can be formed from the same mould. The stair continues up through three storeys in five flights. At the fourth half-landing is a small bull's-eye window providing a glimpse into the hall from high up under the elliptical vault.

The balustrade has a mahogany handrail supported on simple metal rods. The handrail was carved by London specialists in stages: first, a fitting and assembly of raw blocks of timber on site; second, a rough shaping of each block in the workshop; and finally, the assembly and finishing on site – which involved a marvellous, almost balletic performance by a pair of high-spirited Brixton boys with a monstrous boom-box and a pair of unprotected powered routers, hand-held – to achieve the perfect continuous surface from bottom to top. The scroll at the foot of the stair is fitted with an ivory button – the so-called 'mortgage button'. Tradition requires that the button be black if money is outstanding; if the mortgage has been paid off, it is white. There is a gold sovereign secreted under the button.

Such architectural grand gestures often have hidden details of interest, as Bicknell recalls:

> The oval stair leaves various unused volumes (or pockets – hence the Beaux Arts *poché*) in the plan. These are occupied in the two external corners with decorative niches; and in the internal corners by two small rooms – one a washroom and WC, the other a tiny walk-in drinks cabinet with miniature sink and fridge. The cabinet also opens into a corner of the Drawing Room through an almost invisible jib door finished in every detail to match the wall.

The sculptor Simon Verity was commissioned to create a sequence of twelve statues intended to surmount the four porticoes, as a celebration of country life through the seasons. Verity had taken to stone-carving partly

LEFT A breathtaking view of the cantilevered staircase, from the ground floor looking up; it is exhilarating to ascend.

ABOVE LEFT A sketch
by Simon Verity, creator
of the first sculptures
commissioned for the
porticoes, showing
himself at work at
Henbury.

ABOVE RIGHT Although
three of the Verity
sculptures (shown here in
their original positions on
the portico) were carved
to order, they were not in
the end felt right by the
client or Felix Kelly on the
portico, and were instead
placed in the park.

under the influence of his uncle Oliver Hill, and he went on to study with
Robert Baker at Wells Cathedral. Well known for his garden sculpture,
he was also, for many years, director of carving on the West Portal of the
Cathedral of St John the Divine in New York.

At Henbury Hall, each of the four porticoes was to carry three statues,
and each statue was to represent a month, or a sign of the zodiac, grouped
in seasons. The south portico was to hold statues of June, July and August,
modelled on appropriate gods and goddesses representing summer. The
east and west porticoes were to represent spring and autumn, with winter
over the front door on the north face, a two-faced 'January' in the centre.
Verity prepared plasticine models to show how they would work, and then
full-scale timber mock-ups were tried out *in situ*.

In the end, only the three statues for the south portico were completed:
Juno, Apollo and Diana. When they were raised into position, in February
1987, Kelly and Sebastian de Ferranti both felt that they seemed too big in
scale and too baroque in character. Verity himself pointed out, 'Curiously,
no sixteenth-, seventeenth- or eighteenth-century writers except Chambers (who does not clearly tackle the problem) resolve the proper height of
statues on a classical building.'

The commission was terminated – with some sadness, as the correspondence file suggests that Sebastian de Ferranti had hugely enjoyed his
dialogue with Verity – and of the completed figures two were found sites in
the garden and one in the park. Finally, six new cast figures were supplied
by Anna Plowden which were more neoclassical in character; three of them

are sited on the east portico, while on the other pediments there is only one on the crown, which is balanced with neoclassical urns.

The Latin inscription on the frieze of the south portico has a line composed by Professor Jocelyn: 'SEBASTIANVS ZIANI DE FERRANTI VIRTVTE MAIORVM EXAEDIFICAVIT ANNO SALVTIS MDCCCCLXXXVI' – or, in modern English, 'Supported by the virtue of his forefathers, Sebastian Ziani de Ferranti built this house in this year of salvation 1986.' David Kindersley from Cambridge, who had been a pupil of Eric Gill, was considered to carve the inscription, but in the end Richard Grasby from Shaftesbury in Dorset – a remarkable craftsman and scholar, Master of the Art Workers' Guild in 1996 – was selected for the job. Kindersley and his wife, Lida, returned to work on Sir Vincent and Lady de Ferranti's memorial in Henbury churchyard.

The external stone facing finally reached cornice level in November, after the delay in the subcontract caused by the winter of 1984–85. Only a temporary roof covering was possible for the winter of 1985–86 and the leadwork of the porticoes and the permanent roof were not completed until March and April 1986. The roof slopes below the dome were covered with stone flags.

The building, finishing and ornamentation of Henbury was a phenomenon, the sum of many parts. As historians Peter de Figueiredo and Julian Treuherz wrote in *Cheshire Country Houses*: 'Endless trouble was taken over the proportions, necessitating the construction of a beautifully detailed wooden model; even so, during the building work, the silhouette of the dome was raised to create a more substantial impression from ground level. Throughout all these changes de Ferranti played a decisive role. Whilst based on a study of the precedents, Henbury is the result of a collaboration of enthusiasts – artist, architect and patron.'

Bicknell remembers vividly the human story of the construction programme: 'I recall two occasions on which Sebastian entertained all those who worked on the project, firstly when they got the roof on, and then when it was all built; everyone was asked to bring their families; there were three hundred people.'

FOLLOWING PAGES The beauty of Henbury Hall, seen here in its landscape, derives as much from the care in its details as from its overall proportions.

RIGHT A detail of the ornamental carving used for door frames carved by Dick Reid's studio, derived from a model at Beningbrough Hall in Yorkshire.

CHAPTER IX
THE INTERIORS

AS HENBURY HALL ROSE FROM THE GROUND, STILL CURIOUSLY abstract, like a poem of brick and concrete with spaces in between, decorator David Mlinaric was already lined up to work on the interiors. *Mlinaric on Decorating*, written in 2005–2008 with Mirabel Cecil, presents Henbury Hall alongside a Palladian-style house designed by Quinlan Terry and built for the Muse family in Texas. Both are projects where the interior was discussed and planned 'from the beginning of the building work'. These are modern classical houses 'whose design, inside and out, demonstrates how classicism continues to satisfy and be responsive to a certain formal kind of modern living'. Mlinaric's early involvement with the building gives a special clarity to the interiors of Henbury Hall.

Mirabel Cecil interviewed Sebastian de Ferranti, then in his eighties, for the book. He told her: 'If you want to build a house, it's as well to build two first.' She could see how the process 'still fascinates him. He takes an interest in every aspect of the design and decoration, as might be expected from the erstwhile leader of a large international company.' She came away with the feeling that the house had been 'a new and all-encompassing adventure'.

Revisiting Henbury Hall in 2018, Mlinaric said: 'The Henbury Hall project was always enjoyable; the de Ferrantis were so hospitable. I was involved in the very early days, which is always good, and if I can answer the architecture, then I am very pleased. If I can respond to what's given, the jobs are always better.' Mlinaric also remembered meeting Felix Kelly, the originator of the Henbury design. 'I was working on the Chapel at Trinity College, Dublin, and told him about that and he replied, "Oh, you will have to be careful – with God as the client."'

OPPOSITE Interiors of consequence: the enfilade effect of looking from the study through the central great hall and into the morning room.

OPPOSITE, CLOCKWISE
FROM TOP LEFT The
beauty is in the details:
tassels in the dining room;
chinoiserie-style side
tables; one of the lovely
door handles; a detail of
the 'Mme Royale' curtains
in the drawing room.

Choosing David Mlinaric for Henbury Hall shows the quality Sebastian de Ferranti was aiming at in his 'ministry of all the talents'. Mlinaric was widely seen as the star of interior decoration, especially when, after the death of John Fowler in 1979, he began to work on a series of projects for the National Trust, at Beningbrough (which inspired some of the detail at Henbury Hall) and Nostell Priory, in Yorkshire.

His skills are an interesting balance of his artistic eye and meticulous practical work. Born in 1939 to a Yugoslavian father and an English mother, Mlinaric was educated at Downside Abbey and trained at Bartlett School of Architecture, London, where he specialised in interior decoration. He founded David Mlinaric Ltd in 1963 (it became Mlinaric, Henry & Zervudachi Ltd in 1989 – Hugh Henry assisted on the work at Henbury Hall). His practice has been recognised for its original, but subtly traditional, approach to interior design, and much of its work in historic buildings has been based on detailed research.

There are many factors which contribute to a successful interior, and Henbury Hall is a demonstration of the key issues of invention and balance. In 2008, Mirabel Cecil talked of how Mlinaric responded to the architecture of a room: 'Studying the shape of rooms, seeing how the light falls in them and how that affects their architectural details, and how they respond to colours and pattern is crucial in preparing for their decoration.' This is especially true at Henbury Hall, where colours and textiles are orchestrated throughout the house to suit the scale and visual temper of each space. Mlinaric began to visualise all these effects while the rooms were still on paper.

His work for the National Trust in the 1970s and 1980s was especially admired for its ability to make the most of 'barely furnished rooms' in houses that lacked the important collections many people had come to expect. Mlinaric's understanding of architectural form was all-important in such interiors. One feels the same sensitivity at play at Henbury in the cool treatment of the central hall, where the effect is calm and open. Working with the tall Venetian windows specified by Kelly and the inner screen of Ionic columns, the north and south walls seem to dissolve away into the landscape.

At the same time as he was producing interiors for Henbury, Mlinaric was working on the British embassies in Washington, in 1982; and in Paris, in 1983. From 1985 to 1991, he was designing interiors for Lord Rothschild at Spencer House. In the 1990s, he worked at Waddesdon Manor, the Royal Opera House, the National Gallery, and the Victoria and Albert Museum. In 2008, Martin Drury wrote: 'To be a successful interior decorator you must have an artist's eye and a good head for business and a talent for making friends.' When it comes to clients, 'Above all, you must be as interested in the details of their lives as you are in the challenge of what you can do for them.'

There can be little doubt – as evidenced by the dialogue between Julian Bicknell and the de Ferrantis explored above – that Henbury Hall was designed as much around a lifestyle as an idea about a building. It was informed from the start by a highly developed perception of country house living in the late twentieth century, with a mix of indoor/outdoor, formality, intimacy and grandeur, as well as comfort.

FOLLOWING PAGES
The full volume of the
central hall on the *piano
nobile* is a surprise for
visitors; David Mlinaric
advised on the neutral
colour for the walls that
skilfully enhances the
architectural effect.

BELOW Applied overdoor carving shows the cipher of the lily and the ring

Mlinaric recalls, 'The whole project was such fun – always fun. Sebastian was always awake to everything that was going on. I remember doing the layouts for the furnishing of the rooms while I was in Scotland, and I rang Sebastian and said the problem is they are really London-sized rooms.' De Ferranti replied that, in a symmetrical house, it would cost a great deal to make them all larger. Revisiting in 2018, Mlinaric observes, 'Actually I think now they are really Paris-sized rooms.'

According to Mlinaric, 'Sebastian enjoyed the whole business of doing it – I worked very closely with him on every detail. When he liked something, he would make noises of appreciation as if he could taste it – total enthusiasm. The day they moved in there was a proper lunch in the central hall, the table

laid with everything in its place, and a butler – most people manage a sandwich or a takeaway – and as we sat there, you could see that Sebastian just loved it all. Everything was going on around us, and Sebastian was watching it all and then he'd say, "Let's go and see what's going on."'

In Cecil and Mlinaric's 2008 book, the central hall is singled out as the key mediator of the aesthetic:

> The starting point of the interior decoration was the central hall, effectively a grand saloon. It runs from the north to the south portico across the width of the house, as at Millichope and Beningbrough. It is more austerely furnished than either … being used by the family as a sitting room and for entertaining.

RIGHT The extreme height of the doors is an important element of the design.

FOLLOWING PAGES At the south end of the great hall, the window and walls seem to dissolve into the landscape beyond.

ABOVE The Ziani de
Ferranti monogram in
bronze inlay.

OPPOSITE Looking up
into the dome and the
first-floor gallery.

It is austerely coloured and brings the outside in. The walls are painted grey
and the paint tone lightens as the hall ascends … This richly subtle colour
changes from dove grey to buff in certain lights … Natural light comes in
through the double glazed doors.

The decision on the flooring was also key:

I can remember at one point saying, 'Why don't we do the hall floor like that
in the hall at Heveningham?' [The neoclassical hall of Heveningham Hall in
Suffolk is a masterpiece of the architect James Wyatt.] Architect and client
recognised immediately that this would be a good thing to do. The decision
was taken to use native stone, with the Ziani de Ferranti monogram inlaid in
brass under the centre of the dome.

Mlinaric adds that 'The side tables include an original pair, and an iden-
tical pair was made to make a set of four. The lanterns came from Piers von
Westenholz, two small and one large – the chances of that are quite rare.
The lanterns on the landing were copied from a pair which I acquired from
Robert Carrier, the chef, who had them at Hintlesham Hall.'

PREVIOUS PAGES
Looking down from the gallery into the great hall on the *piano nobile*..

ABOVE AND OPPOSITE
The ingenious decoration of the interior of the passenger lift by Paul and Janet Czainski in the spirit of the interior of Brighton Pavilion.

RIGHT The ceiling of the morning room, painted by Hazel Morgan, as if to suggest the classical figures standing on the pediment had gathered to peer into the life of the house below.

The painting and decorating was carried out by M. J. Wyatt (Decorators) Ltd of Bolton. The columns, pilasters and quarter pilasters in the hall were painted in 'Swedish green' scagliola effect by the specialist decorative artist Paul Czainski and his wife, Janet – who also carried out the intense coloured chinoiserie interior of the lift, based on details from a book on the Brighton Pavilion discussed by client and designer in Mlinaric's London office. Of Polish extraction, Czainski was born in Yorkshire and studied Fine Art at Leeds, under Jacob Kramer, and at Goldsmiths, University of London. A leading *trompe l'œil* painter, he has worked on many historic interiors, including Gorhambury House, Spencer House, and the Paris and Brussels embassies. The Czainskis are other members of the 'ministry of all the talents' brought to bear on the interiors of Henbury, contributing to the quality of finish and detail that makes them so memorable. The plinth for a marble sculpture which stands in the window of the dining room, matching the Siena marble of the eighteenth-century chimneypiece (acquired from Mallet's) is another example of Paul Czainski's work.

BELOW The north wall of the dining room, with the Ferneley hunting group portrait adapted by John Ward to include portraits of Sebastian de Ferranti and other members of his family.

RIGHT The dining room chimneypiece is eighteenth-century English; the Fortuny wall hangings and chandelier are both Venetian.

FOLLOWING PAGES The dining room looking through to the drawing room; Henbury Hall was designed around a certain ideal of entertaining.

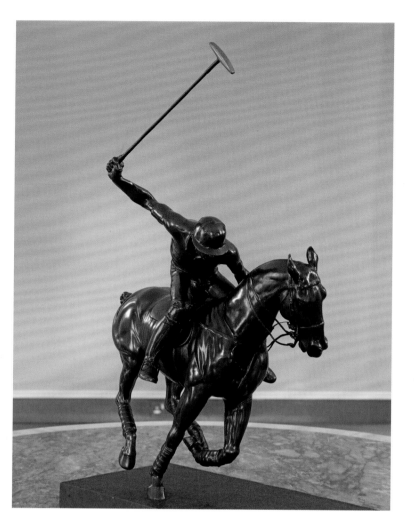

LEFT Horse sculptures around the house attest to the de Ferrantis' love of all things equestrian: hunting and polo especially.

RIGHT The plumed helmet of the 4th/7th Dragoon Guards recalls Sebastian de Ferranti's period as a commissioned officer (serving in Palestine during the Emergency).

The transition from the 'no colour' central space of the great hall – where architectural volume, light and views to the deeply English landscape dominate – to the principal reception rooms has been orchestrated to impressive effect. Both dining room and drawing room have large Serliana windows and high ceilings, but each also has its own notes and character, offering a delightful contrast in tone.

In the dining room, the hospitable heart of the house, there is an unmistakable masculine feel, echoing the country house tradition. The walls are hung with Fortuny 'Glicine Red Museum' fabric, based on a seventeenth-century design, and the room has an appropriately Italian richness. Mlinaric recalls: 'The Fortuny on the walls of the dining room was a nod to Sebastian's Venetian ancestors; and there was a Venetian mirror over an English fireplace and a Venetian Murano chandelier.' The dining room chairs were later replaced by a set which once belonged to Sir Philip Sassoon, acquired from his nephew the Marquess of Cholmondeley.

The magnificent curtains of the dining room, and the other rooms on this floor, were made up by Michael Jewiss, and the braids of the curtains done by Brian Turner. The vast group hunting portrait over the buffet was painted by John Ferneley in the mid-nineteenth century, and the faces altered by John Ward RA for Sebastian de Ferranti so that portraits of himself (in pink coat) and other members of the family replace several of the huntsmen.

On the west side of the house is the lighter-toned, more feminine drawing room with earth-yellow walls. With its comfortable arrangement of sofas and armchairs, this is a room for afternoon tea, pre-lunch and pre-dinner drinks, and conversation. With memorable views over an eighteenth-century park, the theme of nature is picked up in details such as the painted silk cushions and artwork on the walls, including paintings by Lavery and Etty.

OPPOSITE The drawing room looking through to the dining room; Mlinaric chose more feminine colours and fabrics for the drawing room, while the dining room, as is traditional, has a more masculine feel.

BELOW The drawing room chimneypiece: an eighteenth-century original with a central tablet, carved in marble by Dick Reid, of Diana the Huntress.

LEFT AND FOLLOWING
PAGES The drawing
room, on the west side of
the house, has an intimate
but light feel that is
enhanced by the drama
of the high ceilings and
the carefully positioned
paintings.

LEFT AND ABOVE
The study with Sebastian de Ferranti's library chair and desk. The fox cushion was stitched by Sebastian's wife, Gilly, for his birthday, and given to him only ten days before he died.

The fabric chosen for the curtains was described in April 1987 in a letter by Andrea Boscaro of Pauly & Cie as 'named "Mme Royale" … first woven for Marie Antoinette at both Compiègne and Fontainebleu, and rewoven in 1812 for the Grand Trianon at Versailles. I think you are in very good company.' A more recent book suggests it was first woven for the palace of Saint-Cloud in 1797. The curtains are a warp-printed silk and the hang of the drapes is shaped around the Serliana window form.

The inlaid marble chimneypiece is eighteenth-century English, acquired via Mallets, and over it hangs a portrait of a young lady on horseback painted by Edward Seago. Originally a portrait of Lady Woolfson, the face of the young woman riding side-saddle has been altered by John Ward RA into that of one of Sebastian de Ferranti's daughters.

FOLLOWING PAGES.

LEFT The morning room: intimate and comfortable in the south-east corner of the house.

RIGHT The quality of the textures throughout the house is exemplified by the fabrics.

On the south-west corner lies Sebastian de Ferranti's own study-library, designed around a desk already in his possession. Mlinaric recalls that 'We suggested bookcases going into the corner, and Julian designed the bookcases especially. The wallpaper, broad-striped in two greens, was from Coles.' The timber door cases and bookshelves in the study and morning room were both full-on early eighteenth-century designs following the model set by Gibbs, with elaborate cornices, carved mouldings, waterleaf and egg-and-dart all done by Reid's workshop.

The intimate sitting room opposite the library has yellow Fortuny 'Corone' for the curtains, and pale warm brown-yellow paint on the walls. Mlinaric especially picks out one chair in the room: 'The pattern here is a copy of a Louis XIV fabric, after a peacock's eye, supplied by Turnell & Gigon of Chelsea Harbour.'

There was a plan, in the 1980s, for Alan Dodd to paint the oval, coved ceiling in the sitting room 'with sky, urns and flowers' and additional 'grisaille decorations', but this was shelved. In the end, the ceiling was painted in 2005 by Hazel Morgan, a portrait and equestrian painter. Its classical female figures, in grisaille, look down from the blue sky above them as if gazing into a pool. Hazel Morgan recalls: 'Sebastian was a patron and a friend and an adviser; I painted his horses and portraits of his children. He used to climb the scaffolding and would look at it and discuss with me. The figures were intended to read with the figures on the porticoes.'

The 'rustic' ground-floor entrance lobby and the central inner hall are pale grey, with a veined marble chimneypiece, and low free-standing Doric columns painted by Czainski. The bold black doors and skirting were inspired, Mlinaric says, by an eighteenth-century painting of an Irish house interior. Initially, a sculpture group of *The Three Graces* by Edward Hodges Baily stood here; on Sebastian's death, it was acquired by a museum in Taiwan.

Henbury Hall was conceived of as a sociable house, and correspondence files illustrate the enormous care taken to make the relatively low-ceilinged bedrooms elegant and comfortable. Each bedroom suite has its own character, the palette and patterns reflecting a traditional English feel, with strong country themes echoing the colours of nature and the seasons.

The arrangement is brilliantly contrived, with comfortable rooms and convenient facilities; dressing rooms that can serve as single bedrooms, and bathrooms and walk-in clothes closets carved out of the spaces in the porticoes. Bicknell's ingenious design cuts into the side of the porticoes to allow windows in unexpected corners of dressing rooms and bathrooms. Two guest suites occupy the north-west and north-east corners, while the generous master bedroom sequence (including, in effect, two bedrooms, two bathrooms and two dressing rooms) occupies the south. In such a neatly planned environment, the effects of fabric and colour, working with the views over park and gardens, are all-important.

The Sweet Pea Bedroom is hung with 'Sweet Pea' (a Coles paper). The American Bedroom uses a distinctive American stencil print (Liberty), copied from an example in the American wing of the Metropolitan Museum of Art in New York. A 'Williamsburg' stripe wallpaper (in red and brown) is used in the dressing room and bathroom, echoing the feel of the early eighteenth century. The Coles paper 'Victorian Trellis' is used in 'Mrs de Ferranti's bedroom' alongside a handsome 'Hollyhock' chintz for the curtains and bed canopy. Mr de Ferranti's dressing room, with its Regency *bateau au lit*, is curtained and canopied in 'Haseley Acorn'.

The bathrooms are decorated to complement their bedrooms, and every room is hung with watercolours, oils and engravings collected by Sebastian de Ferranti. The master bathroom's antique bath and shower complex was acquired from the London house of the Dowager Marchioness of Cholmondeley. The present Lord Cholmondeley recalls, in 2018, that this bath fitting was 'a typical example of my grandfather's love of gadgets'.

BELOW The entrance hall photographed soon after the house was completed: an ingenious arrangement of an ovoid space, with baseless Doric columns, marbled to match the chimneypiece.

LEFT The principal
bedroom: styled in a very
English spirit.

BELOW LEFT Sebastian
de Ferranti's dressing
room with *bateau au lit*.

Mlinaric devised the wicker screen walls and the ceiling is painted to resemble the sky. Revisiting in 2018, Mlinaric says of the bedroom floor: 'I do like things to be quite simple. Bedrooms ought to be full of little things to look at; the bedrooms here are very pretty and English, a nice contrast to the very architectural "no colour" hall. But the cornices are big-scaled to remind you that this is a proper country house.'

The plasterwork was all executed to a high standard, including, Bicknell recalls, 'very tricky stages – the huge surfaces of the upper gallery with their semicircular blind arches, the lining to the oval stairwell and the elliptical vaults of the great hall. Each of them required meticulous setting out of edge formers and the manipulation of three-metre-long straight edges – all against the clock, since the plaster would set within half an hour or so.'

All the detailed plasterwork – interior columns, architraves, friezes, cornices, impost mouldings, pendentives, the lining to the dome and the coved and domed ceilings of the study and morning room (but excepting the dining room entablature) were precast by Adams Qualityne of Liverpool. Bicknell recalls:

Their workshop was a treasure house of ancient moulds and models – some of them saved, I think, from the fitting out of the *Titanic*.

FOLLOWING PAGES
The image of English country house comfort: the Sweet Pea Bedroom.

BELOW The bathroom, including the bath and shower which Sebastian de Ferranti acquired from the Dowager Marchioness of Cholmondeley.

ABOVE LEFT Looking through to the staircase hall.

ABOVE RIGHT Through the jib door in the dressing room of the Sweet Pea suite.

Most of the work was made directly from our drawings, but the deliciously elaborate frieze in the drawing room was modelled from our outline sketches by a very accomplished sculptor in clay who showed us a set of truly wonderful portrait heads. I learned later that he had gone to India to work with Mother Theresa.

The dining room cornice was supplied and installed by T. E. Ashworth of Leeds, with whom we had worked a few years before at Castle Howard. There we had copied one of the original carved wooden cornices that had escaped the fire of 1945 – a wonderfully elaborate baroque confection with almost rococo double brackets – and remade in plaster for George Howard's newly restored library next to the Garden Hall. We used the same moulds for the dining room at Henbury with single brackets but otherwise the same. Sebastian came back to gild this cornice and the door cases in the dining room some years later.

Other plastering work was done by Horrocks of Liverpool, marblework by W. H. Fraleys & Sons of Birmingham, and metalwork by Richard Quinnell of Surrey.

The interiors as arranged by Mlinaric in the 1980s survive very little altered today (in 2018). The principal difference is the additional gilding in several rooms, including to the plasterwork and side tables in the dining room, which Sebastian de Ferranti had added in the last years of his life. His family used to joke about Sebastian's 'gilt complex', which evidences his affection for the house and shows how design and embellishment became a consuming passion, as he continued to develop this loved and cherished project during his later years.

RIGHT The view from the kitchen window, looking south.

CHAPTER X
THE GARDENS

THE HISTORY OF THE TWELVE ACRES OF GARDENS AT HENBURY stretches back far beyond that of the house – as does that of the wider parkland. Indeed, an awareness of the history of these venerable acres was an important part of the inspiration to design a modern building in classical spirit. This design itself developed out of an early ambition to create something akin to a park pavilion; this later evolved into the design and planning of the house that occupies the site today.

The park was mostly landscaped in the late eighteenth and nineteenth centuries, although one Spanish chestnut near the house has been dated to the seventeenth century. The parkland remains characteristically planted with single trees and clumps and, within these, Sebastian de Ferranti restored rides and created new vistas. The gardens proper, close to the main house but discreetly separate, continue to develop as an evolving part of the Henbury Hall story, building on the bones of what went before. Since 2008, there has been a focused programme to simplify the design, revealing the quality of the natural topography, alongside the vision of the late nineteenth-century garden layout.

There are early mentions, in 1558, of a deer park, fishponds, orchards and hop yards at Henbury. This suggests a well-established and productive garden, although it is not certain that it was on this exact site. Almost a century later, in 1649, when the mansion associated with Henbury was being described as 'a very sumptuous house', mention was made of 'gardens, orchards well stocked with good fruits, dove house'. The main mansion on the site until 1957 seems to date from between 1687 and 1693, with modifications in the 1740s and 1790s and in the nineteenth century.

OPPOSITE The Chinese bridge: designed by Felix Kelly and originally white, it was later painted scarlet and gold.

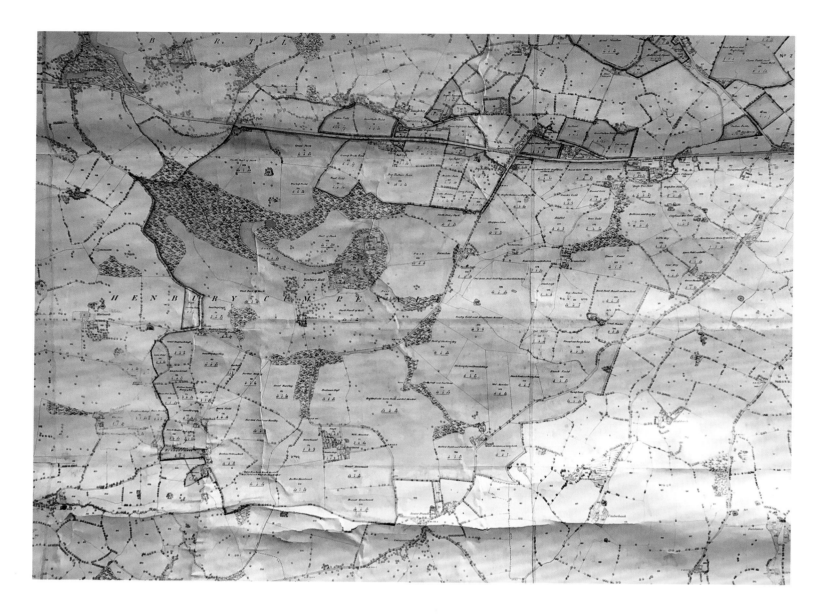

PREVIOUS PAGES
The mature trees of
Henbury Hall give the
house its atmospheric
setting.

The last included a major reduction in the 1850s, and alterations to the stables and barns in the 1880s.

A local tradition concerning the involvement of landscape gardener Humphry Repton (who worked in Cheshire, providing designs for a new lake at Rode Hall in 1790) has never been proven, but a version of the current landscape clearly begins to emerge in the later eighteenth century. In 1727, only the upper lake is visible on estate plans, but the lower lake has been added by the time of the 1794 survey. These great expanses of water, including the third lake which lay below, linked to what is now Big Wood, created a focus for a core area of planting, creating a kind of pleasure ground quite distinct from the immediate setting of the house.

Between 1842 and 1874, when the Henbury estate was owned by the Marsland family, considerable sums appear to have been spent on the garden setting, with 'a series of large pools or reservoirs, well stocked with fish … adding greatly by means of waterfalls and rustic bridges to the beauty of the gardens and shrubberies at the rear of the house.' At the same time as they were reducing the house in the 1850s, the Marslands paid special attention to the estate's productive elements: the 1874 sale particulars reveal the presence of 'a gardener's cottage, greenhouse, peach

ABOVE The estate on the plan of c.1872 – still on a roller in the estate office – showing the extent of the landholding.

and apricot houses, a fern house, pineries, forcing pits, potting sheds, etc.'

Then, in 1874, the estate was bought by the remarkable and wealthy silk manufacturer Thomas Unett Brocklehurst. Outside his work commitments, Brocklehurst was a dedicated traveller, author of *Mexico To-day: A Country with a Great Future, and a Glance at the Prehistoric Remains and Antiquities of the Montezumas* (published in 1883). He reputedly introduced the grey squirrel into the gardens at Henbury – and to the UK. His more celebrated legacy at Henbury was as a tireless plant collector who augmented the grounds with exotic trees and plants acquired during his trips abroad.

ABOVE The lower lake, barns and house seen from above.

Many of the older rhododendron specimens in the garden were imported by him from China. Brocklehurst also added the Foster & Pearson glasshouses to the well-established one-acre walled garden, although the dramatic steep-roofed peach cases against the external south wall are thought to have been installed earlier in the nineteenth century, probably by the Marslands. Brocklehurst also acquired the temple bell that now stands, housed under a small protective tiled roof, near the walled garden and gardener's cottage. He bought it directly from a monastery in Tokyo City during a trip to Japan in 1880.

LEFT The temple bell, acquired for the house in Japan in 1880 by the late-Victorian owner, Thomas Brocklehurst.

LEFT The lime avenue and entrance gates within the park provide a romantic framework for the eastern approach.

The temple it came from was being restored and the monks wanted to install a larger bell. This bell's inscription has been translated as: 'The bell was presented and placed by one Banno Mayo Ho Jo Hinamoto Tesmendga Mura Askusa in the district of Toshena a province of Musashi during the lifetime of a priest named Aluhjung in the month of the year of Hoyea [AD 1700].' The man who cast the bell is named as 'Tenjimara Shigitsuga of Udaganva To Shiro Cit'.

It was from the Brocklehurst family that Sir Vincent de Ferranti bought the Henbury estate in 1957. At that point, the gardens were laid out more or less as you see them today, but were overgrown, with many of the buildings completely derelict – as was so often the case on country estates in the post-war years. Sir Vincent threw himself into the project of restoring the estate, arranging for the gardens to be stocked by Matthews Nurseries of Alderley Edge; this was one of their first major commissions and Mr Matthews made regular visits on Saturday morning, when he would walk

LEFT ABOVE
The gardener's cottage, which stands close to the walled garden.

LEFT BELOW
Orchard trees. .

RIGHT Productive and decorative elements in the vegetable area of the walled garden, developed in the early 2000s. All the vegetables are organically grown.

ABOVE The woodland
canopy is a special feature
of Henbury Hall's setting.

the grounds with Sir Vincent. A large rose garden was developed alongside the walled garden; greenhouses were put fully to use, with carnations and cyclamen cultivated for the house. Fruit, vegetables and flowers for the house (such as sweet peas and gladioli) were planted in the walled garden.

Relatively little of this post-war planting remains today. A major phase of improvement came in the 1980s, when Sebastian de Ferranti was building the present house. He added the Chinese bridge, constructed according to a design for which alternative oil paintings were produced by Felix Kelly. Now bright scarlet and gold, it was originally white. Sebastian de Ferranti also designed the classically inspired brick and stone piers of the tennis court; these carry wires along which nets can be pulled around the court (a pleasing alternative to an unsightly chain link fence).

The glazed pool house next to the court is the work of Francis Machin and features his distinctive ogival shape. The glorious grotto of rocks inside creates a backdrop to a heated pool in the spirit of a classical nymphaeum – Kelly advised on the interior of the pool house. Bicknell observes: 'Francis Machin Senior (one of the sculptors of the Queen's head on the UK coinage) was at work on the rockwork of the pool on one occasion I visited, before work on the house began. He had a tractor with a vast bucket lifting the immense stones into place, as if he was building a drystone wall but at a gigantic size. The result is a triumph, with its waterfall and secret cave below leading to the changing rooms.'

RIGHT Looking across the upper lake towards the entrance gate piers.

CLOCKWISE FROM TOP LEFT The pool house, designed by Francis Machin, with rockwork grotto suggested by Felix Kelly; statue in the pool house; the walled garden seen from the air; the tennis court; gabled brick piers frame the tennis court, and are garlanded with climbing roses.

ABOVE LEFT The 'Uffizi boar' marks part of the circuit route around the lower lake. .

ABOVE RIGHT The woodland path that leads to an eminence known as 'on the top', a favourite viewing point.

Other classical touches include two of the spirited almost baroque-style figures carved by Simon Verity and originally intended for the pediments of the portico, and Gothic arched windows raised over the ram pump house, originally installed in the nineteenth century (before the 1872 Ordnance Survey map). Powered solely by gravity, the pump, by John Blake engineers of Accrington, Lancashire, provided the water for the house and walled garden until the late 1950s, and continues to power the fountain in the garden's lakes and pools.

The 1980s Chinese-style summer house has a pagoda-like roof from which hang bells that ring in the breeze. This little gazebo, with its cosy benches, Murano chandelier and shelves for china, was a great favourite of Prudence and Yolanda, two of Sebastian de Ferranti's elder sisters. In their later years they came to live nearby and walked in the gardens daily; they used to take tea in the gazebo, occasionally surprising their brother on his walks in the garden, as he heard the sound of their laughter ringing from the building. The little gazebo is a beautifully shady spot in summer.

RIGHT The Chinese summer house, framed between two limes.

FOLLOWING PAGES The enclosed Little Garden, with the wider parkland beyond.

ABOVE The Little Garden
provides a sheltered
and elegant area for
entertaining.

FOLLOWING PAGES
The Little Garden sits
against the west end of
the former farm buildings,
and occupies the original
dairy enclosure

An eminence known as 'on the top' is another favourite viewing point; on one side is the upper lake, with the lower lake in front, and the house and descent to wider parkland below. The site is topped with a copy of the Uffizi boar and ringed with old beech trees which link to the 'hanging' bank, restored in 2013. Early summer colour is provided here by two ancient Japanese acers, rhododendrons planted in the nineteenth century, and others acquired from the Rothschild garden at Exbury.

The de Ferrantis continued to introduce trees and flowering shrubs. During the 1980s and 1990s they created the Little Garden, with its round pond, box hedging and shaped yew enclosures. Set in the shelter of brick dairy buildings, which are swathed with white and heavily scented wisteria in the summer, this provides an enchanting enclosure. The spectacular view of the domed rotunda rising above it creates a completely different perspective from those enjoyed from elsewhere in the park. Two delicate weeping pears were moved here in around 2012 to form centrepieces for the box enclosures. This area was originally a pound for gathering cows from the home farm waiting to be milked in the adjoining dairy.

On a couple of occasions, Sebastian de Ferranti suggested adding a chapel in, or next to, this Little Garden. Bicknell recalls: 'I did some sketches for a hexagonal chapel of more or less Gothic type – very small. It would have stood outside the garden but been accessible from it, within sight of the front of the house. But the idea didn't take.

LEFT The view from the enclosed garden looking up at the north-east corner of the house

LEFT AND ABOVE
Mature trees in the parkland:
left, a metasequoia
planted by Thomas Unett
Brocklehurst; above, a
Spanish chestnut over four
hundred years old, from the
original garden around the
old house.

'After his death, I developed a fresh design in a classical manner, repeating the hexagonal plan but in a form distantly derived from Palladio's chapel at Maser or the Mausoleum at Castle Howard. The design served me as a memento of a lovely man and a great time in my life.'

It was never built.

Set in an undulating landscape and surrounding the lower of two magnificent lakes, the gardens of Henbury Hall contain fine specimen trees – Atlantic cedars, Norway spruce and different types of metasequoias – and shrubs, including some rare species of rhododendrons, camellias and magnolias. Since 2008, work has been led by consecutive head gardeners Sean Barton and Steve Smith, with assistance from Katie Heath and Peter Sheridan, and a team of devoted volunteers.

The aim has been to create a more structured landscape, with strong plant groupings that will flourish in the local conditions. Many intensive flower bed plantings have been removed; in others, planting has been hugely reduced to enable 'star plants' to flourish. The more recent changes have been partly inspired by the gardens at Rousham in Oxfordshire, designed by William Kent and one of the most celebrated eighteenth-century gardens in the country.

FOLLOWING PAGES
The box hedging framing
lawn and paved areas in
the eighteenth-century
walled garden.

PREVIOUS PAGES
The interior of the historic
glasshouses; vines and
figs in the former peach
cases, which run along the
south face of the walled
garden.

RIGHT Alliums fill the
border in front of the
peach cases.

FOLLOWING PAGES
A garden enfilade,
suggested by Felix Kelly:
oval openings in the
walled garden, with
inserted sash windows;
the entrance to the
historic ice house.

There is an ambition to increase the collection of fine specimen trees and plants, to add to those already in place, capturing the spirit of the Brocklehursts in the later nineteenth century, as they restored much of the garden from scratch after the devastating floods of 1872. New formal parterre-style beds have been laid out within the brick-walled garden, and a productive and attractive organic vegetable garden built up, keeping the peach cases in use for figs, peaches, apricots and muscat grapes, and the south-facing glasshouses on the north wall for flowers and fruit.

Here, in recent years, a collection of exotics has been established in the tradition founded by Thomas Unett Brocklehurst, focusing mainly on the temperate and tropical *Pteridophytes* and *Orchidaceae*. Former head gardener Sean Barton observes: 'The aim is to gather a Henbury collection of significant botanical importance; highlights of the collection include the large group of *Pamianthe peruviana*, the wonderfully flamboyant amarylid (sadly now extinct in the wild) and the rare *Blechnum palmiforme* from Gough Island in the territory of Tristan da Cunha.'

Espaliered pears form a light division between the current vegetable garden and the parterres, which have an early seventeenth-century flavour in the formality of their patterned pathways. There are more espaliered fruit trees against the walls, including an ancient and much-prized medlar. Set among the tall trees, the walled garden is a hidden world. Sebastian de Ferranti introduced a clever touch in the 1980s, adding a sash window into an oval in the west and south wall, allowing for glimpses of views through. The west-facing aspect of the eastern wall is planted with magnolias that create a handsome show in early summer..

But perhaps the greatest joy of the gardens of Henbury Hall is the way they offer a delectable perambulation around the lower lake. The rising and falling of the ground provides vistas and surprising moments as a visitor completes the circuit, catching sight of follies, columns and statues. Where the eastern head of the lower lake meets the upper lake, there is a cascade framed by a stone bridge supporting the main drive to the house, with a great bank of gunnera rising towards it. Slightly to the north of this lie more specimen trees, a riot of camellias, azaleas and rhododendrons, and a small column that was erected as a memorial to the great flood.

Above this, a hydrangea walk leads the eye back to the dome and lantern over the house. These appear to merge with the great sloping roof of the stables and barns, giving the impression – especially in golden sunshine or glowing sunset – of a painting of a Tuscan village. Between this viewpoint and the walled garden lies a *Prunus subhirtella*, a gift from the late Charlie Brocklehurst, once owner of neighbouring Hare Hill, the garden of which is now owned by the National Trust. He was related to the family who owned Henbury; this tree is always known as 'Charlie's cherry tree'.

Gilly de Ferranti, who has been closely involved in the new phase of the restoration, speaks with special warmth about the gardens. 'The garden at Henbury is an enchanted place. There has been a garden here for hundreds of years, and the atmosphere can be felt of all those who have gone before. In the mornings when the mist rises over the lakes, and in the evenings when the long shadows stretch across the grass, it is as close to paradise as one may be. It is a magical, peaceful place; many visitors remark on it. And for me it is a place of great personal happiness.'

OPPOSITE A hidden corner: *Clematis* 'Broughton Star' growing over sheds.

FOLLOWING PAGES The weir and bridge, seen across the lower lake.

CHAPTER XI

IN CONTEXT:
CLASSICAL CONTINUITY

ARCHITECTURE HAS A NARRATIVE OF ITS OWN. BUILDINGS ARE defined by the designers and makers, but also by those who bring them into being. The 'built narrative' is so often more of a constellation of events than one single dramatic unfolding, more like the night sky than the horizon. Some buildings seem to fully occupy their own stories, to be all the things they were meant to be: Henbury Hall is one such.

The house, with its evocation of the Palladian and classical ideal, was and is seen by many as a statement of traditionalism, an expression of a new conservatism that is a feature of the story of the 1980s. To some extent it is, as a deliberate restatement of the opportunities of classical design, closely linked to the traditions of country house hospitality and the pleasures of the reviving qualities of the country retreat celebrated by authors of the classical world, among them Horace, Pliny and Cicero. Henbury Hall's architecture is, above all, an expression of the villa as an idealised work of architecture which emerged from the thinking of Renaissance architects.

But Henbury Hall was also a statement of individualism, and so perhaps even more an accurate reflection of the late twentieth-century cycle of ideas. It is an expression of the freedom of the individual to ask of life what they want of it, to decide what they want to devote their individual energies to, and to draw together the threads of technology, life experience and aesthetic ideals into a built form for that purpose. For Sebastian de Ferranti, it was a beloved home, a retreat and a place to entertain, and a crafted work of art, in which he strove, with the contributions of artists, to tell of his own profound interest in Venice and the Veneto, and in classical architecture as perceived by Palladio and his eighteenth-century admirers.

PREVIOUS PAGES
Detail of the carved
inscription in the frieze
of the south-facing
portico, with lily-and-ring
keystone and Dick Reid's
special lily capital.

As Julian Bicknell observed in 1987, modern technology opened up a new freedom of choice in architecture as in other walks of life. Sebastian de Ferranti was a technology-minded industrialist who relished the opportunity to choose to build the house that he wanted, to assemble that 'ministry of all the talents' which could make it happen, and to follow the detail of the project's unfolding to a rare, if not unprecedented, degree. This is often where the real joy and wonder of the living classical tradition lies: the visible display of handcrafts, skills, materials, in a building made serviceable and comfortable by modern technology.

On the one hand, it is possible to place the arc of this story in the broader narrative of the quiet – and not so quiet – continuity of the classical tradition in Britain and in the United States. In Britain this tradition was exemplified by John Martin Robinson's book *The Latest Country Houses* (1984) and in the works of architects such as Francis Johnson, Raymond Erith, Quinlan Terry, John Simpson, Craig Hamilton, Robert Adam, Nigel Anderson, Hugh Petter, George Saumarez Smith and Robbie Kerr (the five latter all directors of the ADAM Architecture partnership), Francis Terry, Ptolemy Dean, Stuart Martin, Ben Pentreath Architecture and others. In America, there are many more, including, notable in the residential field, Fairfax and Sammons and Gil Schafer Architects.

There is an important continuity in this story, but it is one that lies not only with the designers but also with those who are prepared to devote energy and funds to commissioning designers. So what we find is that there has always been a clientele, or patron body, who have looked to the classical tradition to root the story of a new country house. This has recently been explored in the author's own book on the ADAM Architecture practice, *The Country House Ideal* (2015), in Mary Miers's *American Houses: The Architecture of Fairfax and Sammons* (2006), and every year in the pages of *Country Life*.

Things have changed a great deal since the 1980s, when Henbury Hall was completed, in the political and social context, but also in architecture and the presence of the classical tradition in the national pysche. In the mid-1990s, Prince Charles's Duchy of Cornwall estates began the famous Poundbury extension to the county town of Dorchester, and in 2003, the new neoclassical Queen's Gallery, attached to Buckingham Palace, designed by John Simpson, was unveiled. The Royal Institute of British Architects now has a designated Traditional Architecture Group for members practising in traditional styles, and in 2010 the RIBA staged an exhibition devoted to the work of three young classicists, George Saumarez Smith, Francis Terry and Ben Pentreath.

Dan Cruickshank wrote of that 2010 exhibition, which highlighted not only the architecture produced by these three classicists, but also the astonishing quality of their draughtsmanship: 'The young designers featured in this exhibition suggest, each in their different ways, that classical architecture is not only culturally rich and beautiful but also relevant and adaptable. Their work is a reminder that one of the constant themes of classicism is to create an architecture that resonates with the human desire for order and harmony, that offers meaning, artistry, ornament and beauty.'

What Cruickshank wrote echoes everything that Sebastian de Ferranti believed and attempted to demonstrate in his great house project.

RIGHT The house
glimpsed through trees,
from the park.

Throughout this story of modern classical architecture, Henbury Hall retains an almost totemic quality, an expression of the best that can be done.

The sheer brio and confidence of Henbury Hall attracted considerable attention at the time of its design; it was celebrated in the postscript to John Martin Robinson's book and included among the dozen post-1960 houses in David Watkin's magisterial *The Classical Country House* (2010), which traces the story from the seventeenth century. John Gummer's clause in the 1997 national planning policy issued by government, which sought to encourage, through planning policy, the commissioning of new country houses of outstanding quality, was inspired by similar stories of estates which had lost the country houses at their centre. Peter de Figueiredo, who co-authored the book on Cheshire country houses published in 1988, revisiting Henbury in 2018, observes that 'Building Henbury in this form was an extraordinarily brave thing to do then, and the house still stands out today.'

The alert and confident presence of such a building in the modern pantheon of late twentieth-century domestic architecture – with all its notable diversity and culture of pushing boundaries of design and technology and 'reaching for the sky' – clearly has given encouragement to others keen to commission such houses, and to promote the alternative approaches of

classical continuity and traditionally inspired design, especially relevant and enjoyable in historic landscape settings.

Clive Aslet, former editor of *Country Life*, who wrote often on the world of the new country house in the 1980s and 1990s, says of Henbury: 'It's exquisite. In lectures, I've sometimes shown a slide of it being built, with cranes over the top – it used to cause gasps of disbelief from the audience, who couldn't believe such a thing could ever be created in the late twentieth century. It also looks perfect in its landscape setting. It was always regarded as one of the jewels of the New Classicism – more romantic than some of the other works of that time, and so always held up as an example of what could be done.'

Above all else, there has to be an acknowledgement of the quality of the crafted object which is Henbury Hall. William Morris was no admirer of the classical tradition, but he might well have admired the degree of involvement of makers of things: masons, joiners, carvers, painters, sculptors and more. The truth is that, while there were differences of opinion, there was real enjoyment and pride in the product. Many regarded the experience as a landmark project in their own lives, and it is an important part of this book to record and pay homage to all of them.

The work was definitely a landmark project for Julian Bicknell, who has gone on to design many private houses, including exacting oak-framed reconstructions of the houses associated with Shakespeare in and around Stratford, and also a remarkable series of commissions in Japan. Bicknell learnt his classicism not in art school (although perspective drawing was still taught at Cambridge when he was a student) but on the job, and his sense and understanding of it was sharpened in the fire-ravaged rooms of the great English masterpiece that is Castle Howard.

In the story of Henbury Hall, there is a strong sense of the patron's deep commitment, a spirit of idealism, self-determination and the sheer enjoyment of 'doing'. One can still imagine Sebastian de Ferranti making the 'noises of appreciation' remembered by David Mlinaric. The story of Henbury Hall is, in the end, the story of one man determining the shape of his house. There are hints at attempts to suggest that the house be modified in the execution, to allow for kitchen suppers and a less formal approach to living, to which the reply came, 'That would be the beginning of the End.'

The mature landscape, partly historic and 'inherited' but partly reshaped by Sebastian de Ferranti, is as important as the architectural centrepiece. The house was designed with the landscape in mind, and the views from rooms and sense of connection with the landscape is critical. The long-established gardens with their mature character also underline that beguiling sense of retreat and exhibit a long narrative of planting, plant collecting and cultivation in nature. The lower lake and its surroundings invite leisurely walks and offer an opportunity to read gardens, house and park from different viewpoints, against different seasons and in different lights. The more recent works on the gardens have been especially respectful of the shaped nature of the place, and governed by an appropriate sense of aesthetic simplicity that also finds its roots in the eighteenth century.

There is a glorious sense of simplicity about the house too: its 'idealised villa' presence teasingly elegant, its plan artfully but intelligently compressed, and the volumes of its interiors in some ways playfully scaled – it is not just a thing to look at, but a home to live in and enjoy. There is theatre in the physical experience of the transfer from the entrance hall, with its stout Doric order and low ceiling, via the subtly Piranesian oval cantilevered staircase, into the expansive, high-ceilinged *piano nobile* with its tranverse great hall space and Ionic order columns. This building is intended to enhance your experience, not merely of the architecture, but of life and the vision of the life well lived. James Lees-Milne visited the house, with the Duchess of Devonshire, in February 1990, and recorded his impression that it was 'stupendous ... the whole house a triumph'.

Donald Buttress, former Surveyor of the Fabric of Westminster Abbey, came to visit with a party led by Julian Bicknell, and wrote in thanks on 23 July 2013, 'The view across the green parkland towards the house in bright sunshine was unforgettable; it was like a glorious jewel-like table centre – a most beautiful casket for living in.' He especially admired the skill 'with which the elegant living spaces were fitted into the overall volume on two or three levels'. Sebastian de Ferranti replied on 1 August, 'The very kind things you say are much appreciated. It is a beautiful and practical place to live in.'

What more is left to say?

OPPOSITE The epitome of the modern stately home: Henbury Hall from the south.

FOLLOWING PAGES
A dream of a place: the long view west from the house.

ACKNOWLEDGEMENTS & REFERENCES

Above all, I am deeply grateful to Gilly de Ferranti for inviting me to write this book, and for being so supportive and hospitable during the whole process (and to James Peill for introducing us); and a special thanks to Robert Dalrymple for his fine design, and to Jo Christian and all the team at Pimpernel Press.

Thanks also to Sue Flack, who has done so much to support the research and administration of this book, and to all at Henbury Hall (Paul Doherty, Pauline Roberts, Philippa Johnson, Agnieszka Domanska) for everything they did to make visits and research possible and enjoyable. Julian Bicknell came to spend two days with me at Henbury, and David Mlinaric, Dick Reid and Paul Czainski all made special visits for me to interview them on site, and Hugo de Ferranti, Camilla de Ferranti and numerous others gave me time and thoughts. The most valuable sources have been the papers and correspondence which remains in the Henbury estate papers in 2018, and a manuscript record of the process written by architectural historian John Martin Robinson, which has proved invaluable.

Thanks too are due to Oliver Bradbury, for his work in the record office on the earlier history of the estate, and Sir Francis Graham-Smith's *Henbury: History of a Village* (2003). Nigel Wilkins was also very helpful in the tracing of 1950s photographs of the old Henbury Hall pre-demolition; the many photographers are credited on page 240, but a special thanks must be made here to Gilly de Ferranti and Sue Flack for sorting out and sharing the images which are in the book, as well as to Susannah Stone, whose picture research and administration has been invaluable. Harriet Salisbury read all my texts, and her proofing advice and editing were masterly. JM

The sources for individual chapters are given below. Every effort has been made to trace copyright holders, but any we have been unable to reach are invited to contact the publishers so full acknowledgement may be given in subsequent editions.

I · HENBURY: A HOUSE IN OUR TIME

Jeremy Musson, 'Henbury Hall, Cheshire', *Country Life* 28 February 2002, 76–81

Donald Bassett, *Fix: the Art and Life of Felix Kelly*, Darrow Press, 2007

John Martin Robinson, *The Latest Country Houses*, Bodley Head, London, 1984, 194–6, quoted on page 23

Letter by Sebastian de Ferranti, 17 March 1998

Letter from Lord Gibson, 1987, quoted in Musson, 2002

II · A COUNTRY ESTATE

John Martin Robinson, *A Guide to the Country Houses of the North-West*, Constable, London, 1991, 42–4, quoted on page 44

Sir Francis Graham-Smith, *Henbury: History of a Village*, Henbury Society, 2003

Cheshire Local Studies and Archives, a survey by Matthias Aston, 1727, D5679/36

Cheshire Local Studies and Archives, an estate survey, 1794, D5678/37

Cheshire Local Studies and Archives, map of 1830

Cheshire Local Studies and Archives, inventory of 1820, D5678/35

Cheshire Local Studies and Archives, D6568/1; and an Indenture, dated 9 May 1687, D5678/1

Cheshire Local Studies and Archives, conveyance of land, D5658/1

Cheshire Local Studies and Archives, sale particulars, Henbury Estate, 1874

Cheshire Local Studies and Archives, estate agents' book, 28/09/1926, inventory dated 12/06/1918, D5678/48

OS Map/1872

Andrew Atherstone, ed., *Bishop J.C. Ryle's Autobiography: The Early Years*, Banner of Truth Trust, Edinburgh 2016, 77–95, quoted on page 38

Mary Crozier, *An Old Silk Family, 1745–1945*, University Press, Aberdeen, 1947

Historic England, National Monuments Record, notes from *c.*1957

Caption on page 39, email from Peter Lee, 3 April 2019

III · FERRANTIS

Amanda Draper, handlist of an exhibition on Ferranti's, n.d.

John F. Wilson, *Ferranti: Building a Family Business, 1882–1975*, Carnegie Publishing Ltd, Lancaster, 1999

IV · SEBASTIAN DE FERRANTI: THE MAN & THE PATRON

2018 author interviews with Hugo de Ferranti, Beatrice Saemann, John Hardy, Ricky Roundell, Sarah Henderson, Randle Brooks, Philippa de Pass, Gilly de Ferranti and Dick Reid

J. M. Brereton, *History of the 4th/7th Royal Dragoon Guards, 1685–1980*, The Regiment, Catterick, 1982

David Charters, *The British Army and Jewish Insurgency in Palestine, 1945–47*, Macmillan, Basingstoke, 1989

The Granada Guildhall Lectures, 1966

Sebastian de Ferranti, obituary, *Daily Telegraph,* 26 October 2015; https://www.telegraph.co.uk/news/obituaries/11939157/Sebastian-de-Ferranti-businessman-obituary.html

V · THE PATH TO HENBURY: PALLADIO & THE PALLADIANS

Bruce Boucher, *Andrea Palladio: The Architect in his Time*, Abbeville Press, New York, 1998, 11-37, 234-6, 290-9, 301-2, 298-9 quoted on page 80

James Ackermann, *Palladio: the Architect and Society,* Penguin, London 1991, 19, 35, 161 quoted on page 75

Robert Tavernor, *Palladio and Palladianism*, Thames & Hudson, London, 1991, 151-80

John Julius Norwich et al., *The Spirit of the Age*, BBC Books, London, 1975, 104-27, 105 quoted on page 78, 110 quoted on page 82

Andrea Palladio, *I quattro libri dell'architettura,* 1570, translated by Isaac Ware as *The Four Books on Architecture*, 1738, republished 1964 by Dover Publications, 41-2, quoted on page 75

Andrea Palladio's architecture in four books, an English translation of *I quattro libri* published in 1736, quoted on page 78

David Watkin, *History of Western Architecture*, Barrie & Jenkins, London, 1986, 12-13, 319, quoted on page 74

David Watkin, *The Classical Country House*, Aurum, London, 2010, 12

Howard Colvin, *Biographical Dictionary of the British Architects: 1600-1840*, Yale University Press, New Haven & London, 2008

Charles Saumarez Smith, *The Building of Castle Howard*, Pimlico, London, 1997, 142-7, 144 quoted on pages 83-84

Sarah Markham, ed., *John Loveday of Caversham: Life and Tours of an Eighteenth Century Onlooker*, Michael Russell Publishing, Salisbury, 1984, 72, quoted on page 84

www.thecountryseat.com

W.B. Neal, *Jefferson's Fine Arts Library*, University of Virginia Press, Charlottesville, 1976

VI · THE DESIGNERS

Dale Allen Guyre, *Minoru Yamasaki: Humanist Architect for a Modernist World*, Yale University Press, New Haven & London, 2017, 261, quoted on page 91

Nigel Woolner, John Taylor, obituary, *Architects' Journal*, 3 September 1988; www.architectsjournal.co.uk/home/obituaries/780211.article

Amanda Harling, obituary of Felix Kelly, *The Independent*, 6 July 1994; https://www.independent.co.uk/news/people/obituary-felix-kelly-1411942.html

Herbert Read, Introduction to *Paintings by Felix Kelly*, Falcon Press, London, 1946, 7-8, quoted on page 96

Donald Bassett, *Fix: The Art and Life of Felix Kelly*, Darrow Press, Auckland, 2007, 13-81, 225-41, esp. 231-6

Peter de Figuerido and Julian Treuherz, *Cheshire Country Houses*, Phillimore, Chichester, 1988, 111-114, 111 quoted on page 99

David Watkin, *Radical Classicism*, Rizzoli, New York, 2006, 9-15, 11 quoted on page 102

Martin Pawley, 'Play it again, Palladio', *The Guardian*, 6 October 1987, 23

Marcus Binney, 'Hooked on Classics', *The Times Magazine*, 28 January 1995, 22-6

VII · THE FINAL DESIGN

Interviews with Julian Bicknell, 2018

John Martin Robinson, MS account of the design and building of Henbury Hall, 1985-6, by kind permission of John Martin Robinson

VIII · BUILDING THE HOUSE

Interviews with Julian Bicknell, Dick Reid, Paul Czainski, 2018, Simon Verity, 2019

Dick Reid, *Chiselling a Living*, Lifebooks, Godalming, 2004

John Cornforth, 'Patriarchs that live in Stone', *Country Life*, 11 March 1999, 80-83

IX · THE INTERIORS

Interviews with David Mlinaric, the Marquess of Cholmondeley, Paul Czainski, Hazel Morgan, 2018

Mirabel Cecil & David Mlinaric, *Mlinaric on Decorating*, Frances Lincoln, London, 2008, 7, 238-46, 7, 238 & 241 quoted on pages 141, 142, 146-7

X · THE GARDENS

Interviews with Gilly de Ferranti, Sean Barton, Steve Smith, 2018

Sir Francis Graham-Smith, *Henbury: History of a Village*, Henbury Society, 2003

XI · IN CONTEXT: CLASSICAL CONTINUITY

Interviews with Clive Aslet, Peter Figueiredo, Julian Treuherz, 2018

John Martin Robinson, *The Latest Country Houses*, Bodley Head, London, 1984, 194-6

Jeremy Musson, *The Country House Ideal*, Merrell, London, 2015

Mary Miers, *American House; The Architecture of Fairfax and Sammons*, Rizzoli, New York, 2006

Dan Cruickshank, *Three Classicists,* Bardwell Press, Cumnor, 2010; and https://www.e-architect.co.uk/exhibitions/three-classicists

James Lees-Milne, *Ceaseless Turmoil*, ed. Michael Bloch, John Murray, London, 2004, 149 quoted on page 230

David Watkin, *The Classical Country House*, Aurum, London, 2010, 12

INDEX

PICTURE CREDITS

Every effort has been made to trace the copyright holders and the publisher apologises for any unintentional omission. We would be pleased to hear from any not acknowledged here and undertake to make all reasonable efforts to include the appropriate credit in any subsequent editions. For permission to reproduce the images below we would like to thank the following.

Agefoto Stock 73 (Clickalps SRLS), 74 (Vdovin Ivan), 76 (Grant Rooney), 80 left (CSP_silviacrisman), 80 right (DEA/A DAGLI ORTI)

Alamy Stock Photo: 50 (Peter Horee); 82 (Peter Lane); 83 (Angelo Hornak)

© Estate of Pietro Annigoni: 60

© Julian Bicknell: jacket back, 105, 106, 109, 110, 114–115, 117, 118 above and below left, 119 below, 120

Bridgeman Images: 68 above left (estate of John Ward, photograph © Robin Forster), 70 (De Agostini Picture Library)

Cheshire Archives and Local Studies: 30, 41 below

© Val Corbett: jacket front, 2–3, 14–15, 28–29, 88–89, 99, 138–139, 190–191, 199 above, 220–22

Country Life Picture Library: 86 (© Paul Barker), 87 right

Ferranti Archives: 50, 51, 52, 54–55, 56, 57, 58 below, 63, 64, 66

© Robin Forster: 33, 62, 154–155

Getty Images: 92 (Bettman)

Henbury Hall Archives: 22, 32, 36, 37, 39, 40, 41 above, 68, 93, 94, 100 below, 122 (© Peter Jenion), 124 left (© Peter Jenion), 124 centre (© Peter Johnson); 124–125 (© Peter Jenion), 125 (© Peter Jenion), 126–127 (© Peter Jenion), 128 (© Peter Jenion), 129 (© Peter Jenion), 130 above left and below right (© Jim Kershaw); 130 above right, centre right and below left (© Dick Reid), 131 (© Dick Reid), 188 (© Jeremy Musson), 222

By kind permission of the estate of Felix Kelly (photographs © Robin Forster): 18, 90, 95, 96, 97, 98, 100 (above), 101

© Location Works 170

© Richard McAlpine: 8–9, 193 above, 199 (below)

© Jim Meads: 68 below

© Ian Moore: 134, 144–145, 147, 158–159, 174–175, 176–177

National Monuments Record: 42–43, 44, 87 left

© National Portrait Gallery: 82 left

© RIBA Collections: 79, 84, 85, 108, 111, 112–113, 116, 118 below right, 119 above

© Pauline Roberts: back flap photograph of plate inscribed by William Mehornay

© Bill Robinson (*The Times*): 104

© William Curtis Rolf: 16, 25, 143 below right, 164–165, 179

© Graham Rust: 1

© Rebecca Sanders: 193 below

© Fritz von der Schulenburg and by kind permission: 135, 136 above right, 173, 178, 182 right, 189, 198 above

© Cally Stockdale: 17, 19, 21, 34–35, 46–47, 48, 53, 59, 132–133, 137, 140, 143 above left, above right, below left, 146, 148–149, 150, 151, 152–153, 156, 157, 160, 161, 162, 163, 166–167, 168–169, 171, 180–181, 182 left, 183, 186–187, 194, 195 above, 197, 198 below, 200 left, 202–203, 206–207, 209, 210–211, 214–215, 224–225, 227, 231, 232–233

By kind permission of the Tarporley Hunt Club: 67 (portraits © Andrew Festing; photographs © A. C. Cooper)

By kind permission of Simon Verity: 136 above left

© Stephen Ward: 12, 20, 26–27, 45, 69, 184, 192, 194 below, 195 centre and below, 196, 200 right, 201, 205, 208, 212, 213 above left, 216, 217, 218, 228–229

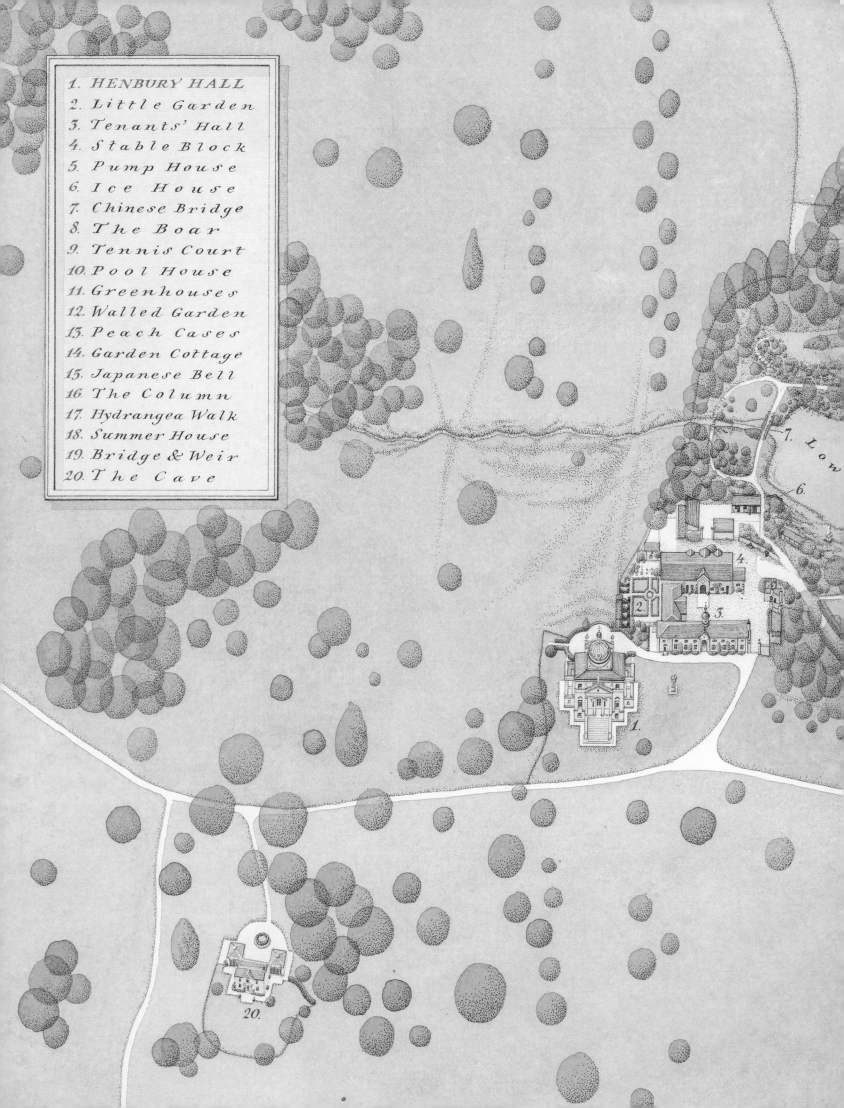

1. HENBURY HALL
2. Little Garden
3. Tenants' Hall
4. Stable Block
5. Pump House
6. Ice House
7. Chinese Bridge
8. The Boar
9. Tennis Court
10. Pool House
11. Greenhouses
12. Walled Garden
13. Peach Cases
14. Garden Cottage
15. Japanese Bell
16. The Column
17. Hydrangea Walk
18. Summer House
19. Bridge & Weir
20. The Cave